SPIRITUAL PRACTICES

Memorial Edition with Reminiscences by His Friends

SWAMI AKHILANANDA

Spiritual Practices

Memorial Edition with Reminiscences by His Friends

by
SWAMI AKHILANANDA

Edited by
Alice May Stark and Claude Alan Stark

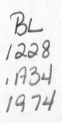

BL
1228
.A34
1974

Claude Stark, Inc.
Cape Cod, Massachusetts 02670

CONTENTS

SWAMI AKHILANANDA

SWAMI AKHILANANDA[1]

by
Claude Alan Stark

"Akhilananda is indeed a jewel amongst his brother monks"

> (From a letter written by Swami Akhandananda
> to Mrs. Anna M. Worcester, December 19, 1934)

Swami Akhilananda was born in East Bengal on February 25, 1894. His mother died when he was still young. Because of the abundance of family members which is usual under the Indian system of family life, he did not lack love in his formative years. His father was a lawyer. His grandfather regularly practiced spiritual disciplines and devotional exercises, and it was from him that Swami, at an early age, first learned the habit of meditation.[2]

He came into contact with several of the swamis of the Ramakrishna Order while in his early teens. Inspired by their lives and example, he decided to devote his own life to the monastic ideal. Before long he developed close association with almost all of the monastic disciples of Sri Ramakrishna. He never met Swami Vivekananda, who had passed into final *samadhi* in 1902. Swami Brahmananda became his teacher. One or two illustrations of his devotion to his *guru* and of his zeal for

---

[1] Excerpted from *God of All: Sri Ramakrishna's Approach to Religious Plurality* by Claude Alan Stark (Cape Cod, Mass.: Claude Stark, Inc.), 1974.

[2] As Gordon Allport writes, "American psychology would improve in richness and wisdom if it accommodated in some way the wise things that [Akhilananda] says about meditation." *Hindu Psychology*, Introduction, p. x.

the spiritual life will bring his training as a monk into sharper focus.

One day when Akhilananda and a brother disciple were walking in the forest with Swami Brahmananda, a tiger appeared at a clearing. Akhilananda and the other disciple both jumped in front of their teacher to protect him from the tiger. Brahmananda, who even at an advanced age was physically very strong, brushed them aside and stood before the tiger, only ten paces away. The teacher and the tiger looked at each other for a few moments. Then the tiger turned and loped away quietly. Akhilananda used to allude to this incident in his lectures and sermons to demonstrate the great love which is the very nature of a fully developed spiritual personality, not only for his disciples, but a universal love which does not stop at human beings alone but includes animals as well, even normally destructive animals (cf. St. Francis and the wolf). The implication was that the tiger felt the great swami's love and fearlessness, and thus turned away and did not molest them.

Another incident of those early days is as follows: Young Akhilananda (Nirode Sannyal) would regularly come to the monastery after school to sit in the presence of his teacher, often without conversation, as would some of the other disciples. One day "Maharaj" said to him, "Hello! I have not seen you for some time. Where have you been?" The boy replied, a little startled: "But, Maharaj, I just came the day before yesterday." With a smile and an impatient gesture, Brahmananda said, "Oh, you and your 'day before yesterday!' "[3]

Swami Premananda was the manager, or "mother," as he was called, of the monastery. He made no formal disciples, yet showered his love and blessings on all the young monks. He had a particular fondness for Akhilananda, for whom he would often prepare a bed in his own room. One day Swami Premananda instructed Akhilananda without further explanation to "study science." Years later Akhilananda gave full credit to Swami Premananda's foresight: "I cannot help remembering

---

[3] From lectures by Akhilananda attended by this writer.

4

what Swami Premananda, one of the great disciples of Sri Ramakrishna, told me in 1915 about studying science."[4] "He used to insist on our study of scientific methods."[5] "He evidently foresaw the world situation and suggested to me to study the contemporary thought-current."[6]

The happiness and contentment that Akhilananda knew during his days as a *brahmacharin* (novice) was complete. He delighted in cooking for his brother monks and for the great swamis. On looking back and speaking of those days, he would disclose that his only desire was to remain a cook in the presence of his master, preparing a variety of Bengali dishes (cf. Brother Lawrence). His only opportunity to continue this activity in the West was on occasions when banquets were held to celebrate the birthday of Sri Ramakrishna. He would spend most of the night cooking huge pots of delicately curried rice, which would be served to the guests along with the catered dinner, customarily held at the University Club in Boston.

After Akhilananda's completion of academic studies at the University of Calcutta in 1919, he had a variety of assignments, one of which was directing flood and famine relief work in South India. He related that he would swim day after day, forging flooded rivers to bring help, accompanied by snakes and crocodiles. At night the villagers would offer him a small bowl of rice, and on, again, he would work the next day. He confided to a group of friends in America, "I can never forget the two young boys who swam along with me, oblivious of the danger. None of us felt any fear."

Then he had the more sedate task of managing a boy's dormitory at a school, and later assisted at the Ramakrishna Center at Madras. During another period he taught philosophy and religion at Annamalai University.

American Experience

In 1926 he left for America. At this point he was offered some

[4] *Modern Problems*, p. 15.
[5] *Hindu Psychology*, p. xvii.
[6] *Modern Problems, loc. cit.*

advice by the then Secretary of the Order, Swami Saradananda. This advice held him in good stead, and he often referred to it to characterize his experience in America. Coming to see him off at the boat along with Swami Akhandananda and others, Swami Saradananda spoke endearingly to him as follows: "I have been to America twice. Learn from my experiences. Some people will praise you to the skies, and glorify you. Others will throw mud on you. Take both equally."

Akhilananda began work immediately. He first founded the center in Providence, Rhode Island, and then in the early forties founded the Boston Center.[7] He kept up both centers, working full time until his death in 1962. The scope of his activities in America was considerable. He travelled country-wide constantly to lecture and attend meetings, and assisted a number of the Ramakrishna Vedanta Societies in this country to keep going in difficult times (e.g., New York, St. Louis, Chicago, Seattle). He attempted to start centers in Philadelphia and Washington, D. C., without success. His main influence, however, was not in center building but in the sphere of character building and intellectual culture. He attracted doctors, philosophers, scientists, professors, psychologists, theologians, sociologists, and students in addition to the average men and women seeking the religious life. He drew them by his sweet nature, loving kindness and sharp intellect.

His bursts of laughter and humorous comments during long, serious conferences are still remembered by those who were present, as the highlight of his company was a wonderful, sparkling sense of humor. This writer attended several such conferences in the early and mid-fifties, such as the Conference on Altruistic Love at the Massachusetts Institute of Technology Auditorium, when Swami Akhilananda was on the platform with Eric Fromm and others, and the Conference on Science,

---

[7] See Paul E. Johnson, *Psychology of Religion* (Nashville, Tenn.: Abingdon Press, 1959), pp. 157-159, for Professor Johnson's description of the worship service he attended at Swami Akhilananda's invitation, on the occasion of the dedication of the Boston Vedanta Center.

6

Philosophy and Religion.[8] We can never forget the quiet, sweet way he sat there, and the good humor he lent the proceedings.

Though a representative of Vedanta to the West, the Swami dressed in traditional Western ministerial garb: clerical collar and black attire. Only on worship days did he put on the ochre robe of the Hindu monk.

Akhilananda was among the pioneers of reverse missionary work, started by Swami Vivekananda in England and America at the turn of the century.[9] Akhilananda was no stranger to Christianity, which has been largely in the custodianship of Western institutions. Early in his spiritual life he developed an intense devotion to Christ while a disciple of Swami Brahmananda. He recalled to some of us the memorable Christmas Eve ceremony at Belur Math when Swami Brahmananda went into *ṣamadhi*, creating an intense spiritual atmosphere. Akhilananda's *Hindu View of Christ* is a landmark in the field, and testifies to his personal devotion and reverence for Jesus. Walter G. Muel-

---

[8] According to the *Providence Evening Bulletin* obituary on September 25, 1962, Akhilananda "was a member of many organizations including the University Club of Boston, Universal Club of Ministers in Rhode Island, Rhode Island World Affairs Council, Rhode Island Philosophical Society, American Philosophical Association, American Academy for the Advancement of Science, American Academy of Political and Social Science, National Association of Biblical Instructors, Oriental Society of America, Foreign Policy Association of America, Fellowship of Reconciliation of America, Conference of Science, Philosophy and Religion, Society for the Scientific Study of Religion, Conference on Religion in a Scientific Age, Institute of Pastoral Care, Religious Education Association, Congress of the Inter-American Psychological Association, American Psychological Association, and American Metaphysical Association. He was vice president and board member of the World Parliament of Religions and was a founding member of the American Foundation of Religion and Psychiatry in New York. He was a charter member of the American Academy of Religion and Mental Health in New York and also was a founding member of the Society of Altruistic Love in America."

[9] See Akhilananda, *Hindu View of Christ*, chap. xii, "Christian Missions," pp. 245-284, especially the following: "We are firmly convinced that sharing of religious experiences should be the basis of missionary activities of any group" (p. 248). "Insofar as a Hindu takes Jesus as the embodiment of divine love in human form, he worships Jesus as veritable God. Therefore, he understands something of the real spirit of Christianity" (pp. 261-262). Cf. also p. 275 ff.

der once commented, "There was a man who *really* understood the New Testament."[10]

In Akhilananda's lectures and books he frequently cited St. Francis, who was among his favorite personalities in the Christian tradition. Once, while in Italy, he visited the chapel where St. Francis had his spiritual experiences, and commented on the atmosphere there. "Not the big cathedral," he remarked, "but the little one around the corner," was the church where he had felt that spirituality still present. He was also especially fond of St. Anthony, to whom he was compared by an intimate friend because he combined intellect and devotion as did the saint of Padua.[11]

Humility was the keynote of Akhilananda's personality. He was humble to the core. At trains or bus stations he would be the last one out. On other occasions, during the automobile ride from Providence to Boston after an evening lecture Sunday night, he would suddenly awaken abruptly from a nap in the back seat and say, "We must get liver for the cats!" No stores were open Sunday night for liver, so upon arrival at Back Bay, the hour nearly midnight and the Swami exhausted from the day's platform work, he would proceed carefully to pick the chicken off some cooked chicken bones so that the two cats could enjoy a chicken dinner instead of canned cat food.

Published Works

Regarding Akhilananda's published works, Professor Hal Bridges of the University of California comments:

Swami Akhilananda—author, it will be remembered, of the

---

[10] Statement made to this writer in May, 1970.

[11] Akhilananda states in this connection: "When an individual is spiritually transformed, his influence affects society tremendously. In fact, the whole ideal of a society is changed. Let us refer to the great mystics of the Middle Ages in Europe. We all know what the condition of Christianity was during their lifetime. If personalities like St. Francis, St. Anthony, and some others had not come at that period, Christianity would have been practically lost without their influence. John Wesley, the founder of the Methodist Church, really saved England from a social revolution. His influence with that of a few others changed the thought current of the people in England." *Hindu View of Christ*, pp. 239-240.

Hindu View of Christ—has published two books expressing mystical thought as psychology. His *Hindu Psychology: Its Meaning for the West* was introduced to American readers in 1946 by Gordon W. Allport of the Harvard psychology department and Edgar Sheffield Brightman of the philosophy department of Boston University. It mingles learned discussion of Western and Hindu psychological theory with unreserved acceptance of the mystical 'superconscious state.' Akhilananda takes issue with Jung for identifying superconscious experiences with the 'deep unconscious state,' describing them as 'vast but dim,' and declaring that they are 'scarcely to be recommended anywhere north of the Tropic of Cancer.' Jung's comment is 'unscientific,' he argues. 'Any man who has had these realizations will laugh at such conclusions.' The superconscious state, samadhi, is not dim, but 'vivid and definite.' North of the Tropic of Cancer it has been recommended by 'Judaeo-Christian types' like St. Teresa and Meister Eckhart who, unlike Jung, speak from experience. And far from its being identical with the unconscious state, it is, in its profound awareness, the very opposite. 'To identify the superconscious state with the unconscious state is to mix darkness and light. In one case man is completely oblivious of the existence of God; in the other case man is fully aware of the existence of God, nay, identified with Him.'

Mysticism also permeated Akhilananda's *Mental Health and Hindu Psychology* (1951). In this study he declares that Hindu psychology grew out of spiritual experience, and is closely related to the mental health field, since the Hindus 'fully realize that until and unless the mind is wholly unified and integrated there is no possibility of spiritual realization or mystical experiences.' He goes on to argue that the fears and anxieties, the conflicts and frustrations that make for mental illness can be overcome by yogic meditation and mystical attainment. Meditation strengthens the will, stabilizes the emotions, and calms the mind, and when mystical experience results it is even more conducive to mental health. The man who truly realizes his oneness with God lives free of negative tensions—in peace and love.[12]

---

[12] Hal Bridges, *American Mysticism, From William James to Zen* (New York: Harper & Row, 1970), pp. 121-122. Used by permission. Professor

The Swami's fourth book, published posthumously, was *Modern Problems and Religion*. It deals with a wide spectrum of personal and communal problems of life, attempting to show how religion best solves these, and that without sincere religious commitment there is no permanent solution. Akhilananda's fifth and final book, published posthumously a decade after his death, was characterized by Dean Muelder as "autobiographical."[13]

When Akhilananda's works were reintroduced in paperback form, Paul E. Johnson wrote, "This is a notable service to bring the Swami's definitive books into circulation again with this new publication, and we hope the clarity of his mind and the radiance of his spirit may in this way bless a continuing circle of readers."[14]

His books did not originate from a desire to publish or from motives of personal ambition as may be the case for some scholars, but from the suggestions of others, namely scholarly friends who felt the Swami had something to share. He worked on them during time snatched from interviews, trips, conferences, letter-writing, and lecturing. His motive was the spirit of service. He did not even keep the rights to the books, but left them in the hands of his publishers, Philosophical Library, Harper Brothers, and Bruce Humphries. His works on Hindu psychology represent a major contribution to scholarship in that the insights of Patanjali's *Yoga Aphorisms* are made understandable and dynamic in the light of modern Western developments in psychology. What is most interesting in these works is Akhilananda's thorough grasp of the history and practice of psychology in the West, from Charcot and Janet to his contemporary times. Yet this was as it should be, as he had prepared himself for it, following the advice of Swami Premananda to study science.

His effectiveness was most pronounced on the personal level with men and women who held the reins of contemporary in-

---

Bridges' book was notably the first survey of its kind "devoted entirely to the history of mysticism in America" (from the flap).

[13] As told to this writer during the summer of 1971.

[14] Letter from Dr. Johnson dated September 22, 1972.

tellectual culture. One day this writer was asked to deliver a small book to a gentleman at Harvard Square—the then greatest living astronomer, Dr. Harlow Shapley. The book was Swami Vivekananda's *Jnana-Yoga*. Subsequently Dr. Shapley reported to the Swami that he carried the book in his pocket everywhere. More than that, Shapley, once an agnostic seeking an answer to the universal dilemma, began touring the country lecturing at universities on science and religion. His book, *Of Stars and Men*,[15] shows the effect of this new direction.

As a Spiritual Teacher

Akhilananda's teaching method was in the tradition of his teacher, Swami Brahmananda, and his teacher's teacher, Sri Ramakrishna. He was always encouraging, never negative. His universality knew no bounds. His understanding of the goal of life was to realize God, and "Love thy neighbor as thyself"[16] was both the path and the result. All religions for him were legitimate ways to attain knowledge and love of God, provided a person is sincere. Speaking to a student with a Catholic background he would turn the person's mind to Jesus or the Madonna.[17] Husband and wife would receive individual instruction and training in religious life, varying with the nature and temperament of each.

Philosophically he was an Advaitist, but an Advaitist who included all forms of personalism. In his second Introduction to *Hindu View of Christ*, Walter G. Muelder writes of the Swami, "His deep appreciation for Christ does not compromise his Vedantist faith that loyalty to Christ is consistent at the practical level with non-dualistic ultimate monism.[18] This did not

---

[15] (Boston: Beacon Press, 1959). Note Akhilananda, *Modern Problems*, p. 66.
[16] Leviticus 19:18.
[17] This writer personally knew of instances when Swami Akhilananda directed Christians back to their churches. His approach may be compared with Swami Bhavyananda of the Ramakrishna Vedanta Centre in London, who was asked by some priests to give them instruction in the technique of meditation. After he gave the instruction, the priests asked what they should meditate on. The Swami's reply was "Jesus, of course."
[18] Pp. xii-xiii.

make him a syncretist, for he fully acknowledged the distinctiveness and worth of each religious tradition. He celebrated with worship ceremonies or special lectures the birthdays of the founders of the world's great religions and commemorated the holy days of Islam and Judaism. He instilled in his students a deep veneration for all religions. As Edgar S. Brightman states in his foreword to *Hindu Psychology*,

> Swami Akhilananda . . . has many friends in educational circles, especially at Brown, Boston, and Harvard Universities. He is welcome among Jews and Christians alike. He is prized both as a scholar and as a religious leader and counselor. It is a great privilege for me to be counted among the friends of this broad-minded and noble man. He is modest, gentle, and tolerant; yet at the same time firm, well-poised, and saintly. . . . The Swami lives by the principles which he . . . recommends to others. . . . The faith which he represents is an outgrowth of the teaching and religious experience of Sri Ramakrishna, a nineteenth-century saint, whose immediate disciple, the Swami Brahmananda, was the teacher of the Swami Akhilananda. To know [him], then, is analogous to knowing one of the early Christians who was separated from Jesus by only one generation.

Temperamentally he was an extremely balanced person. Those who knew him saw him angry only on rare occasions, and then in the spirit of reprimand to students who had committed blunders. His anger then was, as one of the disciples of Sri Ramakrishna had said, "like a line drawn in water: when it is finished, it is gone." When he saw evil, he would either turn away or laugh, but never condemn. He had only sympathy for the suffering of his fellow man. This type of even-mindedness, it may be recalled, is constantly reasserted in the *Bhagavad-Gita* as a primary test of a knower of God.

What was most memorable was his constant selfless spirit, an attitude which was effortless. During the last few years of his life he had various painful illnesses. At one time a condition in his left side was especially bothersome. Yet he continued his round of normal activities: lecturing, travelling, officiating at weddings and funerals, holding dinners and conferences—smiling and laughing, yet holding his side all the while. His comment on the life he was leading in service to God and man was, "A slave is a slave; what can I do?"

This writer once composed the following poem in testimony to Swami Akhilananda's dedicated life, and presented it to him. He read it without a word, and smiled faintly.

Love's Soldier

O wondrous soldier! golden complexioned
   You fight Mother's battles with sympathy's sword.
The war cries—"Struggle! Struggle!
   Struggle to reach That. For That thou art!
Thou art all, and all is One!"—
   Spring from your heart
To urge onward your erring arrowmen.

Your eyes, Sita-like sweet.
   Smile, saddened
By the suffering they see,
   Pierce through misery's veil
Beholding the Spirit breathing in all.

By your loving service to Him
   You teach us, tired divinities,
How to reach the goal.

When we would ask him, in youthful enthusiasm, "What can we do for you, Swami?"—his reply was always, "Live the life, live the life." And if we "lived the life," we would carry out the ideal to which his own life had long ago been fully dedicated, the ideal of Sri Ramakrishna.

SPIRITUAL PRACTICES

INTRODUCTION

Those who know the Vedanta movement are aware that its great leaders explore the whole field of religious experience, particularly mysticism, in the interest of developing the spiritual life. This book is no exception. Swami Akhilananda has followed the method of Sri Ramakrishna and Swami Brahmananda in drawing on all the major living religious traditions as resources for knowledge and instruction in meditation and spiritual development. His earlier writings have shown him to be at home in mystical writings and practices of the Christian saints as well as those of the East and the Middle East in non-Christian cultures. From all serious and mature religious consciousness he draws encouragement and offers guidance to those who will experiment in the fruitfulness of meditation.

This a practical book, not primarily a theoretical treatise. It is an introductory volume comprising primarily a number of closely related lectures on spiritual practices and their meaning. The author soberly and kindly sets to one side those superstitions and magical approaches to religious life which constitute a barrier to effective growth and to modern men's quest for ultimate meaning. He invites minds who are steeped in modern science to begin a spiritual venture which will transform their personalities without betraying their legitimate sophistication. He asks for open-mindedness.

Though drawing on a world-wide range of mystical experiences and writings, Swami Akhilananda does not devote much attention to the exegesis of the texts or passages which he occasionally quotes. These writings are freely used and often make a point in the context of this volume to which an exegetical theologian might not give his assent. This fact does not constitute a major problem because the passages cited are not used as proof-texts so much as allusions or illustrations. Similarities and analogies are stressed more than differences among the traditions, mystics, or thinkers cited. The function is practical rather than theoretical, as we have already noted.

Some Christian readers of this volume will take exception to the author's description and interpretation of certain concepts and doctrines. His references to Augustine, the Reformers, Barth, and Niebuhr are nonetheless interesting, for they help to sharpen the point of view which he develops. The meaning and nature of sin in the Calvinist tradition and in Wesley may be understood differently by their adherents from the way they appear in the Swami's universalistic perspective. Many will wish to enter into a dialogue with him here. The issues cannot be lightly brushed over, since the analysis of man's predicament and salvation has an important bearing on the type of spiritual discipline and the methods of spiritual practices which are appropriate.

Swami Akhilananda does not urge the same design or method of religious devotion for all people. Here he is much wiser and sounder than those guides who recommend the same formula to achieve what is called peace of mind or peace of soul. Mankind embraces many different levels of psychological development and types of temperament. Men embrace many cultural forms and habits. The religious guide or spiritual counselor will be doing well to understand the varieties of religious experience, the levels of growth, and the range of symbolic needs which his disciples, followers, students, or congregations embrace. For each distinctive group an appropriate method or discipline should be developed.

Variety of spiritual practices is justified because it tends to an eventual focus of consciousness. The starting point may be different but meditation is not a mere relativism of foci of attention. Meditation requires the concentration of consciousness. It requires that man withdraw his mind from sense objects and focus his consciousness on God, more particularly on some aspect of God. In religious meditation, symbols, pictures, icons and the like are used to help the mind concentrate on God. These are not objects of thought but rather windows by means of which consciousness directs itself beyond the finitude of present space and time.

In an age of "hidden persuaders" and manipulation, sound religion must constantly protest against bogus mysticism and spiritual short cuts. Intellectual honesty, moral integrity, and religious concentration must go together to form a truthful whole. Simulated effects through mechanical methods and psychological tricks must be repudiated. Prayer has great power, but its power evaporates when it loses contact with reality. Devotees in all religions will appreciate the Swami's devotion to Reality. The reader will realize more fully that the "objective of religion is the awareness of God in our everyday life."

1962

Since the first introduction to this book was written, Swami Akhilananda's death has terminated the valuable practical counsel and guidance in spiritual matters which characterized his leadership in the Vedanta movement. I look back on years of close friendship with him with special gratitude and can only wish that many who will read this book with profit could have felt the spiritual power of his personal solicitude.

Edgar S. Brightman, my principal teacher in matters religious —also a close friend of Swami Akhilananda—in introducing his students to the study of classics of religious mysticism commended four questions which should always be addressed to the work of a mystic: (a) what was the preparation for the experience? (b) how was the experience described? (c) what was the philosophical or theological interpretation of the experience? and (d) what were the fruits of the experience? If these four questions are kept in mind in reading about spiritual practices and the Swami's own experience, the reader will be enriched by the reality of devotion. In the pursuit of the spiritually practical he will sense the presence of the eternal.

1972

WALTER G. MUELDER
Dean, Boston University School of Theology
Boston, Massachusetts

ON CONCURRENTLY HEARING BERLIOZ'
L'ENFANCE DU CHRIST AND
READING THE SWAMI AKHILANANDA

(for Alice and Claude Stark)

Windows are opening from a mysterious source:
From the quiet pages of this book a spirit calls,
Declaring the glory of all human faiths
And their essential unity in the cosmic quest.

This Hindu would surely perceive and adore my Christ,
And, like the shepherds in Berlioz, say:
"May he wax, may he prosper;
Dear Child, may God bless you."

When I make Christmas after the Advent time,
I shall be companied by a friendly sage:
A Swami from the East will sing a hymn
In cognizance of my own Lord's Nativity.

December 16, 1973

KENDIG BRUBAKER CULLY
Former Dean, New York Theological Seminary
New York, New York

PREFACE

My good friend Dr. Clarence Faust is really responsible for this book. Some time ago he insisted on my writing a book on spiritual practices. He also repeatedly told me there is a need of such a book in our contemporary society. As he used to urge me to do whenever he met me, I gave a series of lectures on these topics forming the various chapters in the book.

It is needless to say that there is considerable confusion in the minds of many thinkers regarding religion itself. They often think that it is nothing but a bundle of superstitions based on infantile dependence. We admit that there are types of persons who have this kind of attitude toward religion. But this is not the whole of religion. There are others who seem to think a man can become religious if he is associated with some religious institution or organization. Again, there are others who seem to feel that spiritual practices as they will be expounded in the book are not meant for modern Western people. We have to say frankly that their conclusions are erroneous. A person cannot become a religious person merely by being associated with an organization. He must try to live his life according to the basic principles of religion.

The word mysticism is also very much misunderstood by a great many persons in the West. Mysticism is not a kind of hallucination or imagination, but it is direct and immediate experience of God or Ultimate Reality. There are some valid characteristics of authentic mystic experience, as we shall find in the chapter on mysticism. Some people think that mysticism can be induced by mechanical means. They have a completely erroneous understanding of mysticism. Mechanical methods cannot give us direct and immediate experience of God. They may produce certain states of mind which are not spiritual experience. Even superficial observation of the behavior of the persons who practice mechanical methods will convince us that such methods cannot produce what St. Francis, St. Teresa, St. John of the Cross, Jakob Boehme, Hans Denck, John Wesley, Ruysbroeck, and others had in the Christian tradition. The experiences of Jewish Hasidic and Cabalistic mystics, Hindu mystics, Buddhist mystics, and Sufi Islamic mystics will convince us that there is a world of difference between real mysticism and the state of mind which is produced by mechanical means.

My good friend Dr. Faust insisted on my writing a book, knowing the necessity of a clear understanding of religion and also knowing the value of religious practices. We are very grateful to him that he understands the present condition of religious life of the people. We also feel that we should answer some of the most important questions regarding religion and its application in life.

Some people believe that we do not need any search after God or Absolute; we must live an ethical life and do humanistic work. Ethical culture and humanism are not the goal of what we call religion. They are necessary for the fulfillment of religion and they are needed as the foundation of religious culture. But the goal of religion is the attainment of knowledge of the Ultimate Reality and its relationship with finite beings. Real religion should teach us how to become aware of the Absolute or God or Holy One or Allah or Brahman or Truth.

When we study the lives and activities of the founders and great saints and sages of different religions, we find that all of them became fully aware of this Ultimate Reality. Again, there are some persons in the contemporary world who think that there is no possibility of becoming aware of Reality through spiritual practices. According to them, revelation comes from God. It is He who gives everything and we have to depend on Him. Our answer to them is: it is true that real knowledge or revelation comes from God, yet we have to prepare ourselves for that realization. Herein lies the utility of various practices. Great religious leaders of all the great religions taught different techniques of spiritual development according to their traditions. In the Hindu tradition they declare that every individual has a unique mind, even though common elements are found in different minds. So the Hindus prescribe various techniques for the realization of God, suitable to different structures of mind. Though they may seem to be different, yet they lead different individuals to the same goal. That is the very reason Sri Ramakrishna, who was born in 1836 and passed away in 1886, verified different techniques according to Hindu systems of thought and also according to other great religions. And He declared that all these methods are valid and lead us to the same state of superconscious experience of the Ultimate Reality. He gives a very interesting illustration. These religions are something like different doorways to a huge building. Anyone can enter into this building by opening up any of these doors.

We had the great privilege of knowing most of the disciples of Sri Ramakrishna and of living with them. We observed that they went through spiritual practices and insisted on our doing intense spiritual practices. It is true that in the history of mankind there are a few cases of persons who had a sudden revelation, but all other great spiritual personalities belonging to the great religions like Christianity, Judaism, Hinduism, Islam, Buddhism, and Taoism, verified the Ultimate Reality through their intense practices. We had the privilege of knowing such dynamic spiritual leaders, so that in the book we have given many references from their teachings and activities. It does not mean that we ignore the effectiveness of the teachings of other spiritual leaders belonging to different religions, but it means only that we had direct contact with these personalities and we learned from them. Because of their love, we were attracted to them and we tried to follow those methods. So we like to share these ideas with others.

We admit that there are persons who seek religion for health, wealth, and prosperity, or to get rid of sorrow and sufferings. But there are also persons who want to really know God; as Jesus said, "First seek the Kingdom of God." Spiritual practices are needed for all these three types of persons. Even the persons who have a petitioning type of religion must also train their minds to have effective prayer. Of course, the primary objective of religious practices is to know and love God and fellowbeings. It also has a pragmatic and practical effect in life and in our human relationships. In the contemporary world many persons are suffering from emotional disturbances and psychosomatic diseases. It is practically impossible to overcome them without proper understanding of the values of spiritual practices and their application in life. So from various points of view, spiritual practices are essential for harmonious and peaceful living.

Most of the chapters of the book are no doubt devoted to individual spiritual practices. The last chapter shows how the spiritual man can become a help to society in solving contemporary social, national, international, and interracial problems. We want to make it clear that though this book emphasizes spiritual practices, yet our intention is also to show that a spiritual man who has real experience of God is a true lover of mankind and can do very effective welfare work in our contemporary world. We are convinced that unless a man goes through spiritual discipline, he cannot remain an effective welfare worker. It is true that early Buddhists did not even discuss God. Yet Buddha emphasized the Eightfold Path of Life, which includes right living, right action, and right meditation. Buddhists could keep up humanism for so many centuries because they emphasized the practice of meditation along with humanitarian work and such other activities.

We are indeed very grateful to Dr. Faust for his persistent requests and for reading the manuscript. Dr. Edwin Booth and Dr. Paul Johnson of Boston University; Dr. Gordon Allport, Dr. James Adams, and Dr. George Williams of Harvard University; Dr. Dana Farnsworth, Head of the Health Department of Harvard University; Dr. Houston Shrader of Nazarene College, Massachusetts; Dr. Allen E. Claxton of New York Methodist Church; Dean Walter H. Clark of Hartford Theological Seminary; and Dr. O. Hobart Mowrer of Illinois University read the manuscript and gave valuable suggestions. Some of the Swamis of the Ramakrishna Order in America also were kind enough to read the manuscript. We are very grateful to our friend Dean Muelder for writing the Introduction.

The real credit for this book goes to my beloved teacher, Swami Brahmananda, to the founder of our Order, Swami Vivekananda, and to other great disciples of Sri Ramakrishna, for their teachings, love, and inspiration. If there is any credit for this humble work, it certainly goes to them. May this book be useful and serviceable to the real seekers after Truth belonging to different religious traditions.

AKHILANANDA
1962

REQUIREMENTS OF A SPIRITUAL STUDENT

We are often asked about the qualities required in a spiritual student. It is our conviction that any man or woman—Christian, Hindu, Muslim, Jew, Buddhist, Taoist, agnostic, or atheist—can have spiritual realization, provided he fulfills certain requirements. A great scientist of this country related to us a conversation he had with Einstein, who told him: "I do not have a glimpse of the Absolute but Eddington has it." We had met Eddington in India during 1937 when he accompanied a Calcutta scientist to our monastery. From his facial expression then we had the distinct impression that he was on the borderline of spiritual realization. Our friend, the American scientist, asked, "Swami, can we scientists have a glimpse of the Absolute?" The answer was, "Yes, positively. Your minds are being trained in scientific study and research. To know the Absolute, you merely have to change the object of your concentration."

A question may arise about those who have sudden spiritual experiences without fulfilling the requirements for spiritual training as we technically understand it. Take, for instance, St. Paul. He hated Jesus; yet he had spiritual realization and experience of Jesus on the way to Damascus. As a result, he was thoroughly changed. In fact, he was in a sense the founder of Christianity. When St. Francis of Assisi returned from a military expedition in Sicily, he went to a church and had exalted spiritual realization. He was born the son of a merchant and as a young man had a good time dancing, singing, making merry. After his spiritual experience, he was so thoroughly changed that he could not go back to his home or indulge in his former pleasurable activities. We find similar instances in the lives of St. Augustine and St. Ignatius. The same is also true of some persons in the Indian tradition. However, the majority of mystics and spiritual leaders belonging to the different religions have had to fulfill the requirements for spiritual training before attaining religious realization. It is not that spiritual enlightenment is exclusive to any one religious group or to any particular individual. Any person of any race, religion, or creed can reach this goal, provided that he or she fulfills the requirements of a spiritual student.

God is not the exclusive property of anyone. It is a mistake for anyone to think that if he follows a certain creed or doctrine, or if he is associated with a certain religious group, he alone can know God. Every person has the right to experience God; He is the universal Being and is present everywhere. Did not Jesus say that "The Kingdom of God is within?" St. Paul said, "Ye are the children of God and joint heirs with Christ." Hindus declare, "Thou art That; thou art That." The Buddhists say: "Truth is within you." The Sufi Islamic devotees have the same idea: "The Deity is within." Similar expressions are used by the great Jewish leaders, Cabalistic and others. So all persons have the potentiality for realizing God.

Some religious leaders of the West seem to think that human beings cannot do anything about attaining divine revelation or spiritual experience, as they must wait for the grace of God. When we study the lives of the great spiritual personalities belonging to the different great religions, we find that they have gone through certain spiritual practices, thereby fulfilling the requirements for realization of God. We do, indeed, understand the place of the grace of God in spiritual experiences. It is of vital importance. People may like to talk about the grace of God; yet, if they do not prepare themselves for the enjoyment of His grace, they cannot have it. Sri Ramakrishna used to give a pertinent illustration of this:

> The wind of God's grace is incessantly blowing. Lazy sailors on this sea of life do not take advantage of it. But the active and the strong always keep their minds unfurled to catch the friendly breeze, and thus reach their destination very soon.[1]

---

[1] *Sayings of Sri Ramakrishna* (3rd ed.; Mylapore, Madras: Sri Ramakrishna Math, 1925), XXVI: 533.

Now what are the requirements of the spiritual student? In the first place, he must have a desire to know God. Without this, he cannot realize God. In the Vedanta Aphorisms of the Hindu sacred literature it is declared, "Now, then, the question of Brahman [God] arises." What is the meaning of the word "then"? It means that when a person has the four required qualities, then the question about God arises in the mind. In other words, there must be a desire to know God.

This desire can arise in various ways. Some individuals feel inadequate in life. They cannot face their problems nor can they solve them. Disease, death, changing conditions, uncertainty, all sorts of problems exist. So help is sought from a supernatural Being or God to remove these conditions. Their motive is not to know God but to get help from Him.

Others approach God and go to church, synagogue, or temple to pray for money, power, position, even victory in war. We have found that although the motives of some of these people are not very exalted they can still change because they are at least thinking of God. From that they develop a desire to know God. We can give Saul as an example. Before he became St. Paul he hated Jesus intensely. If you love a man you think of him. If you hate a man you think of him. In either case the effect is there. If a person touches fire either consciously or unconsciously he is burned. So, to think of an incarnation of God means to be transformed.

A third group of people desire to know God because they are inquisitive by nature. They want to know what is behind this finite and changeable world. They want to know what is beyond the limitations of mere theological knowledge or philosophical interpretation. Take, for instance, our friend the scientist. He has a keen, brilliant mind and he wants to know what is really real. He wants to know what is behind the galaxies or the changeable conditions of the galaxies. Some are not so educated but still have a peculiar attraction to God. There was a poor, uneducated man in India who had a desire to know God, and he experienced the highest spiritual realization. Even some of the so-called untouchable castes have attained this exalted state. One of the disciples of Sri Ramakrishna was illiterate. He could not even pronounce the alphabet of his own language. Yet he had the highest spiritual experiences because a strong desire for that fulfillment had been aroused in him. We knew him very well and found him to be an exalted spiritual personality.

The second requirement of a spiritual student is that he must have a discriminative faculty. Without this he cannot carry out the prescribed and correct methods for realizing God. As we know, there are many persons who are indiscriminate and move about from one group to another seeking the sensational. An outstanding psychologist reported to us that there are such groups functioning in the vicinity of Los Angeles with various enticements. Unstable people are attracted to them because they do not have discrimination and they do not understand what is the proper method for attainment of knowledge. They are fooled by the sensational and the promise of quick results with easy methods. They want self-glorification, control of the laws of nature, and so on.

The third requirement is that the spiritual student must have the power to carry out the methods that are reasonable and suitable for him. If he does not have such power or tenacity, he cannot reach God. He must have also the ability to avoid activities that are really harmful for his spiritual realization. Of course, one cannot have this power overnight. We do know that inordinate tendencies of anger, envy, or jealousy are great obstacles. However, the spiritual aspirant must struggle to overcome and remove these obstacles. Then alone can he develop his higher tendencies. If he does not have the desire, right understanding, and the power to struggle, he cannot grow spiritually.

The fourth requirement is the cultivation of spiritual qualities like sympathy, love, patience, endurance, and purity. Again we must say that a person cannot reach the goal overnight. Most people have some degree of destructive tendencies, or inordinate affections, to use the terminology of Thomas à Kempis. Human minds are not like automobiles which can be brought to an immediate stop. Thus one cannot instantaneously get rid of hatred. Only in very rare cases have there been immediate changes. So it is necessary to accept and cultivate ethical principles, step by step. This requires much patience and courage. Without such qualities a person becomes despondent. If a man hates another, he should acknowledge it as a weakness. It is important for a man to recognize these tendencies within himself and to know that they are obstacles to his spiritual progress. Then he must struggle to change himself and develop his mind.

Patanjali, the founder of Hindu psychology in about 300 B.C., made it clear that the human mind must be rebuilt with positive, constructive, and healthy tendencies. He says that one should cultivate love, sympathy, humility, and forgiveness, in order to overcome pride and egoism. "Friendship, mercy, gladness, and indifference, being thought of in regard to subjects, happy, unhappy, good, and evil respectively, pacify the Chitta [mind-stuff]."[2] Swami Vivekananda says of this aphorism:

> We must have these four sorts of ideas. We must have friendship for all; we must be merciful towards those that are in misery; when people are happy we ought to be happy, and to the wicked we must be indifferent. So with all subjects that come before us. If the subject is a good one, we shall feel friendly towards it; if the subject of thought is one that is miserable we must be merciful towards the subject. If it is good we must be glad, if it is evil we must be indifferent. These attitudes of the mind towards the different subjects that come before it will make the mind peaceful. . . . It is not that we lose by thus restraining ourselves; we are gaining infinitely more than we suspect. Each time we suppress hatred, or a feeling of anger, it is so much good energy stored up in our favour; that piece of energy will be converted into the higher powers.[3]

As we shall mention in the chapter on "Requirements of a Spiritual Teacher," Swami Brahmananda always advocated rebuilding the mind with constructive tendencies. He warned his

---

[2] *The Complete Works of Swami Vivekananda* (Mayavati, Almora, Himalayas: Advaita Ashrama, 1931), I, 222.

[3] *Ibid.*, pp. 222-223.

students against despondency and always encouraged them in spite of their weaknesses. We saw the tremendous changes that took place in some individuals under his guidance in spite of their discouragement and disheartening experiences with thoughtless and jealous persons. One young man that we know seemed about to be crushed by some designing people. However, he had tremendous faith in the loving spiritual care of Swami Brahmananda and wholly trusted him, relying on his love and judgment. Without mentioning the destructive activities, but fully aware of what was going on, Swami Brahmananda greatly encouraged his young disciple. Because of the boy's complete trust in his teacher, this turned out to be a blessing to him and his spiritual growth.

Let us cite examples of two great Christian leaders: St. Francis of Assisi and St. John of the Cross. What terrible humiliation they suffered! Yet they never became despondent or discouraged. The results were unique, as we know from history. We can cite other incidents and examples of encouragement and enthusiasm for spiritual growth in spite of severe humiliation and cruelty. So we are not making theoretical statements; rather they are based on valid experiences in the human history of spiritual growth.

Another essential requirement of a spiritual student is that he must be willing to perform religious practices. Without these he cannot grow. As he cannot experience God or realize the highest truth immediately, he must steadily practice under the guidance of a real spiritual teacher. It is most important for him to tenaciously continue the practices; then alone will he become really fit for spiritual life. Otherwise, the mind will remain restless; and in this state the mind cannot experience God.

So tenacity and patience constitute another requirement for the student. We know how people act. They go to a church, synagogue, temple, or spiritual teacher for a little while. Then they lose their enthusiasm and give up when they do not have immediate results. Perseverance is one of the most important requirements for spiritual growth. When any of Swami Brahmananda's disciples used to complain to him: "Maharaj, the mind is so restless," he would smile and encourage him to continue his practices steadily. He told some of us that until a person practices steadily for about two years, he would not even listen to their complaints because he knew that it takes time for the mind to change. So under the guidance of a spiritual teacher perseverance is necessary. To use the words of Swami Brahmananda: "Slow but steady; slow but steady." With this steadiness, the restless mind will be transformed. Then comes the highest realization, as we explain in the chapter titled "What is Mysticism?"

2

REQUIREMENTS OF A SPIRITUAL TEACHER

There is considerable confusion in the minds of many persons regarding the requirements of a spiritual teacher. Some think that if a man talks about God, reads about God, discusses philosophy, or interprets theology, he is a religious teacher. Some people think, also, that if anyone accepts certain doctrines, dogmas, or creeds, or performs rituals and ceremonies, he becomes a spiritual teacher.

There are certain basic requirements for a spiritual teacher. It is not necessary for him to have mere intellectual culture and achievement, or philosophical and theological understanding. Of course, philosophical and theological discourses convince us about the existence of God and the values of religion. We do not minimize the importance of such discussions, nor do we minimize the importance of rituals, ceremonies or the acceptance of certain aspects or values of religion. They have significance but they are not the real requirement of a spiritual teacher.

Many persons think that if they belong to certain groups or accept certain doctrines they can have students or they can convert people; they can take people to the fold through the acceptance of doctrine. Nowadays, in the Western countries, particularly in America and certain parts of Europe, people have what they call "mass conversion." Now, the question arises: Can this kind of acceptance, enthusiasm, or emotional expression really convert anyone or really give spiritual rebirth? Our answer is, no. The basic requirements of a teacher are to be found in his own spiritual life. He may not have philosophical or formal theological understanding. But if he lives a spiritual life and integrates his emotions, then alone he can become a teacher.

There are different types of teachers. According to Indian tradition, the first class of teachers are incarnations of God. Incarnations of God have the power to illumine instantaneously any man or any woman at any time. A person does not have to go through any spiritual training to be illumined if he is blessed enough to be present when an incarnation comes to this world. The disciples of Jesus had direct and immediate experience of God. They did not have to accept any creeds, doctrines, or dogmas. Yet, because of His own spiritual illumination, Jesus could transmit that power to others instantaneously. We happen to know also similar instances in the lives of other great personalities, such as Krishna and Buddha.

Just about a century ago, there lived a great spiritual personality in India, Sri Ramakrishna, who is regarded as an incarnation of God. In 1886, on the first day of January, some of His lay followers went to see Him. Among them were doctors, writers, businessmen, bankers, lawyers, and householders. Sri Ramakrishna came out of His room and went to the garden to walk, while a number of persons followed Him. He said to them: "Ah, this dramatist and this doctor say this man is an incarnation of God (referring to himself). What do they know?" The dramatist to whom he referred was Girish Ghosh, who is considered greater than Shakespeare. Girish came forward and knelt humbly at Sri Ramakrishna's feet, saying, "What can I know of you?" At once, Sri Ramakrishna entered a high exalted mood. He touched the forehead of this man; instantaneously the great dramatist entered into what we call a superconscious state. And then one after another the people came forward and knelt before Him and He touched their forehead or their chests. At once they had the highest spiritual realization. These people whom we call incarnations of God can give direct experience of God immediately and instantaneously. As we know, Jesus did not discriminate against anyone. To Mary Magdalene, Peter, John, to all sorts of people, whether they were agriculturists, bankers, or fishermen, he gave the highest realization. Incarnations have the power to transmit spiritual illumination to anyone.

The second class of teachers have a similar type of power. They generally come with the incarnations of God, and in the Indian religious tradition we call them eternally free souls. Although they have power similar to that of an incarnation, the difference is that they have to be in a particular mood to transmit it. So if a person happens to be present at the time they are in that exalted mood, he can have high spiritual realizations. We happened to be present on one occasion when a number of persons attended a ceremony performed by Swami Brahmananda. He was dedicating an educational institution of our Order. At that time hundreds of people were present—bankers, lawyers, politicians, laborers, and average men and women. He was in such an exalted mood that all persons felt a tremendous spiritual power or vibration. Some also had high spiritual realization. We do know that on certain occasions when Swami Brahmananda was in an exalted mood, he just looked at a person and said, "Hello, So and So." That was enough; at once the individual experienced spiritual realization. We happened to be present many times when this happened. I have seen also on different occasions that other great disciples of Sri Ramakrishna, such as Swami Premananda, transmitted spiritual force. We do know also what happened in the life of Swami Vivekananda, how he changed, transformed, and gave spiritual realization to many persons, even those together in groups. On one occasion a young professor of philosophy went to visit him in Madras. He arrived while the great Swami was sitting quietly, absorbed in a high spiritual state. A few scholars and devotees were gathered around him; but they did not feel inclined to disturb him and were also sitting quietly. The young professor came into the room and saluted Swami Vivekananda by touching his feet, in Indian fashion. This startled the Swami and he exclaimed, "What have you done! Everything is over for you!" From that day on the young man was thoroughly changed. He was formerly a follower of the English skeptic philosophers and he used to argue with Swami Vivekananda. But after his experience he could no longer continue his former ways of life. He gave up his professional work and teaching and led an intensely spiritual life. A very prominent doctor, devoted to Swami Vivekananda, took care of him and his family. The transformation was amazing. We had the pleasure of knowing his wife and children at a later date. Many persons had exalted spiritual realization in America, Europe, and India in the presence of this great Swami. From these experiences we can easily understand what Jesus, Buddha, or Krishna did in previous centuries.

The third class of teachers are those who have experienced God, but they do not have the same type of power as those in the first two classes. They can give guidance and help, but the students have to cooperate with them. In other words, certain spiritual discipline and training is necessary under their guidance. Then the attainment of spiritual realization is possible.

The fourth class of teachers are those who have at times a glimpse of the Reality, or perhaps not even that. Yet they are living a life of spiritual discipline and they are going through intense spiritual practices. They are struggling for realization of God but they are not yet well established in the experience of God. However, they can help others provided both teacher and student go through spiritual practices regularly.

Now, these four classes of teachers can *really* guide us. Then again, we can say there is another group of people, not so intensely spiritual but sincere nevertheless, who are trying to meditate and perform devotional exercises and who can also give guidance and help. They can say: "I go through these practices. I find peace of mind, and satisfaction. If you do the same, you can also have some experiences." We admit, the fifth class of teachers cannot give us the direct experience of God. But still they can help us.

Now, the first and most important requirement in a spiritual teacher is his spiritual life. If he performs spiritual practices, meditates, and goes through devotional exercises, then alone he can help others, because he understands life and knows how to live. He does not have to be an intellectual person, nor does he have to know philosophy or theology.

The second requirement is that a teacher must have deep sympathy and love for the students. Of course, it goes without saying that if a man experiences God, he becomes a lover of mankind, even of animals, and all creatures. He cannot do anything harmful. He cannot become emotionally upset; he loves all living beings. Now, this is the link, so to speak, between teacher and student. If the teacher loves a student, has sympathy for him, then we will find he can transmit spiritual help to his student. The student may not be just now really fit; he may not be willing to go through spiritual practices; or may have many inordinate tendencies. Yet if the teacher loves him, he cannot help feel a pull toward God. We have seen time and again that because of the love of a teacher, people are transformed. But if a teacher adopts an authoritarian attitude, such as, "If you do not follow my instructions then you will be punished," he only antagonizes the student or makes him afraid. I once heard a very sad report. A young girl was in a hospital with a serious case of typhoid. The girl was almost in a hopeless condition. A spiritual teacher came to her and wanted to perform a religious ritual. The girl, though very sick, strictly followed the orders of the doctor. The teacher wanted to do something which the girl refused to accept, as it was contrary to the doctor's wishes. The shocking thing was that the teacher at once condemned her and said, "You will go to hell." Can such persons inspire anyone? Can they give real spiritual awakening, not to speak of spiritual realization? Certainly not. On the other hand, St. Francis of Assisi could not hate or condemn even destructive animals. He went to the wolf of Gubbio and said, "Brother Wolf, don't kill the goats." And Brother Wolf stopped killing the goats. See the difference! He could love even a wolf! Similar instances are found in all religious traditions. If we study the lives of the great Jewish, Christian, Hindu, and Sufi Islamic mystics, we will find that all of them were centers of love. They could inspire people by their living examples, and above all, by their love.

We noticed how the Holy Mother, Sri Sarada Devi, transformed extremely disorganized persons by her love. She treated them as her own children and poured out her love and sympathy to them. Some questionable persons went to Swami

Vivekananda when he was in the West. Instead of treating them as sinful people he treated them with love and sympathy. They were transformed into saintly personalities. We personally experienced the influence of Swami Brahmananda, Swami Premananda, and others. An actress went to see Swami Brahmananda but she did not have the courage to enter his presence. Her sense of guilt and inadequacy made her embarrassed. But Swami Brahmananda went forward and invited her into his presence, giving her loving care and even food. A few days of such contact changed this woman in such a way that she could not continue with her old way of life and she intensified her spiritual practices. In 1923, we were amazed to find her staying in a holy place only a few years after her first visit to this great Swami. She was devoting her whole time and energy to spiritual practices and she became a saintly woman. We can cite other cases of this type in connection with Swami Brahmananda. Similar incidents occurred in the presence of and in association with Swami Premananda and other great disciples of Sri Ramakrishna. We are thoroughly convinced that it is love and sympathy on the part of the teacher that can transform even destructive and demoralized persons. It is no matter whether a spiritual person belongs to this or that religious group. What really matters is that he loves and sympathizes with his students, disciples, or counsellees.

The third requirement is patience on the part of the teacher. A spiritual teacher must be extremely patient. We do know human weaknesses, and we know how human minds behave. Suppose a spiritual teacher gives instructions to a student; do you think he can at once change his mind? He may be inspired; he may get temporary enthusiasm. But so far as the mind is concerned, it takes time to be changed. That is the very reason we say the teacher must be patient. The teacher must understand the requirements of the disciple or student and know that he cannot change overnight. If the teacher expects the student to do so, he is mistaken. In fact, to be frank, a teacher is like a mother. As you know, a real mother has tremendous patience with her children. Similarly, a spiritual teacher must have tremendous patience with his or her students. He knows human beings cannot change suddenly; but he knows that with love and patience, he can gradually change the personality of the student. This is a very important factor.

It was amazing to us to know how Sri Sarada Devi, the Holy Mother, would treat even disorganized persons. Once, a young Swami was complaining to her about the behavior of another person. She only listened. She did not say anything. The young man asked, "What do you say, Mother?" Her answer was: "What can I say? I am the Mother." She knew fully that human beings do not overcome their weaknesses and defects immediately. On another occasion, a young man was doing something very undesirable in the Holy Mother's presence. She turned her face away from him in order to avoid seeing it. We also happen to know of similar instances when she treated different individuals with patience and forgiveness and thereby changed their personality.

We can relate many episodes from the life of Swami Brahmananda. On a particular occasion two men were actually fighting each other in a holy place. He withdrew himself from the place as if he did not notice it. Being the Head of the Order, he could have taken a very strong disciplinary action. Instead, he instantly went to his room and became absorbed in God. This very act made these fellows extremely embarrassed and changed their behavior pattern. We know many episodes of a very serious nature when he removed conflict and stopped hateful activities by being patient and by asking those persons to intensify their spiritual practices. He would often say that it is very easy to drive people away by rigidity, but it is impossible to pull them in by this method. On one occasion, he told us: "If I tell certain things to such-and-such a person, he will go away." I was amazed how he handled that situation with deep love, sympathy, and patience.

Then again, a teacher must have also a clear understanding of the needs of the student. Herein lies the utility of what we call intuitive or even rational understanding of the requirements of the student. If a teacher does not understand these, he cannot give real guidance. Every student is different. If we think the world can be spiritualized in just one way, we are mistaken. A real spiritual teacher knows the needs of the minds of different students, and he gives instruction and advice according to their needs, not according to one type only.

He understands that there are some who are extremely rational and others who are devotional, active, or meditative. If the teacher does not have insight into the nature of his students and does not understand the structure of their minds, and if he tries to force one particular pattern of practice and mental attitude on all students, he will create serious impediments to their growth. In such a way he can really drive many of his students away from religious practices. Sir Arthur Keith of England, in a book titled *I Believe*,[4] wrote a vivid account of his reasons for giving up orthodox Scottish Presbyterianism. It could not satisfy his rational mentality. He said that if he had to follow any religion it would be Buddhism or something similar. He had this reaction because he was not satisfied with the type of practices advocated in his own church. He needed a rational type of religion. In our humble experiences of counselling, we definitely found that the students with a predominantly intellectual type of mentality cannot be forced to take up devotional spiritual practices. There are some who cannot take the personal aspect of God, as in the devotional method; rather they have to use the symbol of the impersonal aspect of God and follow the rational method.

So we say that real spiritual awakening or real spiritual guidance should be given individually, according to the requirements of each student. A real spiritual teacher who has the experience of God cannot help having this insight. He has depth of understanding. He knows the nature and the structure of the minds of the different students, and he guides them accordingly. We have seen amazing instances of this when we came in contact with our own beloved teacher. We saw how he gave instructions and guidance to different individuals according to

---

[4] Sir Arthur Keith, *I Believe* (New York: Simon and Schuster, 1939).

their requirements. From this we can easily understand how other great spiritual personalities taught their disciples. Do we not know how Jesus trained or treated His different disciples? Do we not know how Buddha treated his disciples according to their requirements? Do we not know how Sri Ramakrishna treated or trained His disciples? It is interesting to note that among the disciples of Sri Ramakrishna who had highest spiritual realizations even when they were boys, there were considerable differences in the structures of their minds. Sri Ramakrishna guided each one of them according to his own particular structure and they also became great teachers.

Let us take, for instance, Swami Vivekananda. His mind was predominantly rational. He followed that path primarily, but he was also a lover of God. His love cannot be measured by ordinary people. He attained various types of *samadhi* (superconscious experience) even though he started first with the monistic attitude. In contrast, Swami Brahmananda was extremely devotional. But afterward, he also had various types of *samadhi*. We do know that other disciples of Sri Ramakrishna had their own individual tendencies. Some were ritualistic, some active, and so on. Yet all of them had the highest spiritual realization.

So a teacher must guide us according to our own requirements. Real teachers are not only patient and enduring, but they have also deeper understanding of the nature of their students. That is the very reason they can endure even the weaknesses of their students, knowing that they will come out of them gradually. Only the incarnations can change people instantly. So we say, if we find these qualities in a teacher:—that he is emotionally integrated, that he does not have any hateful feelings, that he does not change with environmental changes, —then we know that he is a spiritual man.

Of course, one question may arise here: How can we know that a man has experienced God? We do know that a man of God is an integrated person. His personality is stable. He is thoroughly unified. The conditions or events of life do not change him. Suppose a Hitler or a Mussolini appears. Do you think a real spiritual teacher would be affected by Hitler? Why should he come to the level of Hitler, or become destructive? He cannot do so. So we find that a real spiritual teacher is a thoroughly integrated person. Because of his spiritual realization, his mind is extremely dynamic and at the same time unified. So when we find that a person is integrated and his emotions are steady and stable, then we become convinced that he has some religious experience, otherwise he could not behave this way. St. Francis, St. Augustine, St. Ignatius, St. Teresa, St. John of the Cross, George Fox, John Wesley, Ruysbroeck —these great personalities in the Christian tradition had high spiritual realization. The same is true of many in other religious traditions. Of course, we do not know how they experienced it, but we do have evidence of their behavior and their influence on the world. According to their behavior, their personality, and the effect of their personality, we are convinced that they were men of God. When we find a teacher that has such a dynamic personality or the deeper understanding of our nature, as well as sympathy, love, patience, endurance, and forgiveness, then we can depend on him and we can be sure to have real inspiration from him.

Forgiveness is to be emphasized also. A spiritual teacher who has high spiritual realization or experience of God knows human nature. Knowing this, he actually forgives the weaknesses of the individual. He knows human beings are like this for the time being. Instead of disliking those who have inordinate tendencies, he loves them just the same, forgives them just the same, and ignores their weaknesses. He encourages them to take a positive method. We cannot help thinking of Swami Brahmananda's method. We never heard him saying to anyone, "Don't do it. Don't do it." He always would put his advice in a positive way: "Do this. Do this. Do this." The idea was, as we see it now, that the more one intensifies one's spiritual practices, the more one becomes interested in God, the less he will have those inordinate tendencies. As Sri Ramakrishna used to say, the more you go toward Benares, the farther away is Calcutta. Or we can say, the more you go toward New York, the farther away is Boston. Similarly, the more we intensify our spiritual practices, the more these weaknesses or inordinate tendencies drop off. A spiritual teacher knows it, and knowing this, he never says a word of discouragement. He always encourages: "Go ahead, go ahead, go ahead." When we find these qualities in a spiritual teacher, we cannot help thinking: "Ah, this man or this woman can help us." In fact, they are the people who can transform others, who can awaken spiritual consciousness in others—nay, who can even give the experience of God.

3

DO WE NEED RELIGION?

The word "religion" creates various responses in the people of the contemporary world. Some individuals react to it with definite antagonism and hostility. On the other hand, some show an extreme form of dependence on religion without a clear understanding of its real meaning and purpose. Swami Vivekananda clarifies this when he says:

> Of all the forces that have worked and are still working to mould the destinies of the human race, none, certainly, is more potent than that, the manifestation of which we call religion. All social organizations have somewhere in their background the workings of that force; and the greatest cohesive impulses ever brought into play among human units have been derived from this power. It is obvious to all of us that the bonds of religion often have proved stronger than the bonds of race, nationality, or even family. It is a well-known fact that persons worshipping the same God, believing in the same religion, have stood by each other with much greater strength and constancy than people of merely the same family descent, or even brothers. . . . *Man is man so long as he is struggling to rise above nature*, and this nature is both internal and external.[5]

There is a serious question in the minds of many persons: Do we need religion? We are told by leaders of different religious groups that it is necessary for everyone. Some of them say that without it we shall go to hell. On the other hand, extremists contend that we do not need religion because it has been the cause of much trouble in the world.

My good friend, Dr. Gordon Allport, had an interesting conversation with two Indian scholars, a husband and wife, who were supposed to be social scientists. They were discussing re-

---

[5] Swami Vivekananda, *Works*, II, 57 ff.

ligion in general, as well as Hinduism, which the couple told Dr. Allport is "nothing but magic and superstition." He replied to them, "That is not the whole of Hinduism." He, an American scholar, had to explain this to an Indian couple! We cannot blame them alone; there are many Indians who think the same because they do not know the ABC's of real Hinduism. Similar conclusions are made about other great religions of the world.

Utilitarians say that we need not accept the supernatural being or God. We can live an ethical or humanistic life. They know what happened in Europe in the name of religion, so we cannot blame the utilitarians or humanists of the West for thinking as they do. Unfortunately, in the name of religion, people have been exploited, as the great British thinker, R. H. Tawney, explains. In his writings he describes how Christianity was used in the Middle Ages by the feudal lords, in the Reformation era by the princes, and then by the capitalists for their own advantage. He says:

> Religion has been converted from the keystone which holds together the social edifice into one department within it, and the idea of a rule of right is replaced by economic expediency as the arbiter of policy and the criterion of conduct. From a spiritual being, who, in order to survive, must devote a reasonable attention to economic interest, man seems sometimes to have become an economic animal, who will be prudent, nevertheless, if he takes due precautions to assure his spiritual well-being.[6]

Not only the humanists, but also other scholars of Europe, the philosophers and scientists, advocated pragmatism. "Do not talk about the supernatural being. It is enough to live a pragmatic and ethical life. We must have ethics to avoid conflict and destruction of society." This is a good attitude: live an ethical life; be humanists; help your neighbors; stabilize your society. However, the humanists cannot meet all the needs of society.

---

[6] R. H. Tawney, *Religion and the Rise of Capitalism* (New York: Harcourt Brace and Co., Inc., 1947), p. 246.

This is where religion comes in. With religion all human needs can be fulfilled.

Recently, Julian Huxley wrote a book, *Religion Without Revelation*, in which he attempted to prove that revelation or experience of God is not necessary in religion. He concluded that a humanistic society is sufficient for mankind. This great scientist means well; however, he does not understand the real purpose of religion. Nor does he understand that ethical culture or humanism cannot stand without the search for the real goal of religion: to manifest the divinity in man, and to feel the presence of God in everything.

Similarly, Bertrand Russell, the great English philosopher and thinker, published a book, *Why I Am Not a Christian*. He not only criticizes Christianity but he also criticizes other religions in a very superficial way with sweeping statements, indicating that he is not acquainted with their philosophy and values. He should at least have a clear understanding of real Christianity.

We understand why these thinkers express such ideas and we cannot blame them. However, as scientists, they should apply scientific methods of careful investigation and valid reasoning in order to evaluate truly the purpose and meaning of religion.

Other extremists, the materialists, such as Karl Marx, Engels, Feuerbach, and their followers, seriously condemned religion. They did not have a well-defined code of ethics like the utilitarians or pragmatists; but they had an ethical approach in their feeling for the poor and their attempts to help them. They, too, felt that religion had done great harm to society, so they advocated that it is enough to live a good life and help one's neighbors. Their idea was that one should not eat cake without first giving cake to his neighbor.

Freud, Watson, Pavlov, and such others, criticized religion also. Along with Marxists and others they said that it creates superstition, hallucination, repression, prejudice, authoritarianism, exploitation of people, and dependence. Every one of these words should be carefully defined and properly understood.

We admit that the critics are right in condemning certain abuses in the name of religion; but these practices and activities do not represent the true meaning of religion as defined by Swami Vivekananda or advocated by the great founders of the world's religions. We do know that critics study only the abuses; but they should thoroughly investigate the true meaning of religion and evaluate it without preconceived notions, presuppositions, and superstitions. Recently a psychiatrist of the orthodox Freudian school told a college boy that valid religious experiences are hallucinations. We must say that he has not even crossed the threshold of religious knowledge; yet he has come to this conclusion without understanding the meaning of religion and its dynamic power.

Many modern social scientists study and glorify the ideas of Watson or Freud. Dr. Pitirim A. Sorokin often says that they want to make a Jesus out of Freud. However, Freud cannot be blamed wholly for his feeling against religion. We learned from Dr. Viktor Frankl, a Viennese psychiatrist who recently visited this country, and from biographical material, that Freud suffered some very unpleasant experiences caused by so-called religious leaders. Naturally, he thought that religion itself created the trouble, as it gave him so much pain. He developed bitterness and disgust. Then he rationalized his feelings in terms of his philosophy—that religion creates repression; the superego, which is created by religion, social customs, and traditions, represses the natural, normal tendencies and keeps them hidden in the *id* or unconscious, where they create trouble. We should also remember that Freud observed only abnormal patients, which did not help him to be an objective and dispassionate observer of normal religious manifestations.[7]

Some psychiatrists, clergymen, and chaplains conclude that in order to be a clergyman one must receive psychiatric treatment. A prominent psychiatrist of New York City, who is advisor to a religious denomination in this country, is of the opin-

---

[7] Swami Akhilananda, *Mental Health and Hindu Psychology* (New York: Harper & Bros., 1951).

ion that in order to satisfy their neurotic needs men and women enter the ministry or turn to religion. We admit that there are individuals who become ministers or turn to a religious life because of emotional disturbances or neuroses of various types. But to make the sweeping generalization that all of them are neurotic or disturbed is erroneous, superficial, and unscientific. If this psychiatrist properly understands the meaning of religion, he cannot scientifically come to this conclusion. Religion is not for neurotic satisfaction; it is the means for the attainment of knowledge of the Ultimate Reality or God. There are many persons who become ministers or other kinds of religious teachers because they want to know the Truth and to share it with others.

In order to understand the need for religion, we must have a clear understanding of what it is. People function on different levels of development. The real religious teachers take into consideration the particular mental constitution and requirements of their students and give them religious training according to their tendencies and capacity, step by step, so that they can reach gradually the ultimate goal of religion. Then they can understand what real religion is.

Some people seek religion for health, wealth, and prosperity. For instance, in spite of the wonderful advance of modern medicine and in spite of the skeptical attitude toward religion in this scientific age, innumerable persons try to find health through religion. A university dean and his wife told us about the many religious health cults in California, particularly in the vicinity of Los Angeles. They are to be found in other cities also. We know intimately a few Christian ministers who genuinely feel that they must heal the sick through their religious practices or prayers. One minister in Baltimore has been doing this for some time. He is a sincere and good man with a great heart. Many people are anxious to be healed in this manner. However, that is their only intention in religion. They want to get rid of physical ailments. Some also want to get rid of other disturbing and painful elements in their lives through the intervention of a supernatural Being. We find that there are two types of people

48

in this group: one who wants to get rid of pain and agony and the other who asks for something to be given to him—negative and positive aspects. The second type prays for success, wealth, power, position, even victory in war, and so on. However, approaches to God for these various reasons are not the real purpose of religion.

Another group consists of those who are curious about death and departed relatives or friends. A minister of my acquaintance had a unique experience which was verified as valid. The small daughter of one of his devoted parishioners was very sick and he stayed with her for two or three days praying for her recovery. Finally, the child died. She was seen after her death by another parishioner and narrated things that happened just before her death, which were known only to herself and the minister. There are scholars in this country, like Professor C. J. Ducasse and others, who try to establish the validity of departed souls and who are convinced of their existence.

There are many spiritualist churches or groups throughout the United States. Many persons are interested in departed souls, in spite of the scientific achievements, rationalism, and skepticism in society today. Even Sir Oliver Lodge, a great English scientist, became interested in the existence of departed souls because his son died. We cannot blame anyone for that. We admit there are departed souls and that one can see them, although there are fraudulent cases. We know of valid instances which were thoroughly investigated and verified. However, the acceptance of the existence of departed souls is not a necessary adjunct of real religion, even though religious persons may see them.

There is another group of persons who perform so-called magic. They float on air, walk on water or fire, remain buried underground, and so on. They think that because they can do these things they are religious; and people are fascinated by them. "Oh, how wonderful!" they exclaim. Of late, quite a few thinkers have challenged us about Jesus, as He demonstrated supernatural, extraordinary powers over matter. "If these powers are not representative of true religion, how can you say that

49

Jesus was a great religious personality?" they ask. We reply that we must remember to whom He was teaching religion. They were on different levels of development. It was for their development that He performed the miracles and then led them to higher values of religion. In the Sermon on the Mount and elsewhere He spoke the highest truths: "Blessed are the pure in heart, for they shall see God." "Thou shalt love thy God with all thy heart." "Thou shalt love thy neighbor as thyself."

There is a great deal of interest in extrasensory perception (ESP). It does not necessarily indicate knowledge of the Reality. There is an Indian in this country who claims he is a *yogi*. A woman told us he is troubling her through his thought transference and influence. She became frightened by physical disturbances. One cannot be sure whether the man is responsible or whether she developed the symptoms herself. However, even if this man has the power to influence the minds of others, does it mean that he is religious? Hypnotism is practiced, but one does not have to be religious to do it. One gentleman of our acquaintance has been helping disturbed people through hypnosis. Many psychiatrists use this method, but it does not necessarily mean that they are religious.

Swami Vivekananda said that real religion is the "manifestation of the divinity that is already in man." It is the love of God and love of neighbor. It is the attainment of the knowledge of the truth, as Buddha declared. It is the attainment of the knowledge of the Deity that is within you, as the Sufi Islamic people declared. Real religion is the knowledge of God, or the Kingdom of God, within.

There are some who may say: "We have our homes, automobiles, television, and such other things. Why do we need religion?" They do not know that there is an inherent urge in man to find out who he is. He wants to know whether there is a permanent Reality behind this changeable world. In 1956, an outstanding scientist of this country gave a lecture at the conference of the Institute of Religion in the Age of Science, which was being held on Star Island. He severely criticized religion. The chairman of the session, another great scientist, called on me for a comment. I smiled at the speaker and asked him, "Do you ever ask yourself, 'Who am I? Will there be anything left after I die? Is there anything permanent in me?'" "Of course!" he answered, and smiled too. "Of course I think about it." Then I asked him, "Do you also wonder if there is something real, really real, behind this phenomenal world, behind the changeable entities like ice, snow, water, vapor?" "Of course," he said, "I want to know." "You are not an atheist, as you have tried to establish," I told him. "You are an agnostic or skeptic. That is all you can say. Rather it seems you are a Buddhist." He began to laugh at this and replied, "Did you notice that I did not criticize Buddhism?"

Some time or other, this desire to know who we are comes to us. We may be allured by the things that we see—television, cars, clothes, and so on; but sooner or later the question arises: "Is there anything within me which lives forever?" Sir Oliver Lodge wanted to know what happened to his son, Raymond, when he died. This was the beginning of his psychical research. Then he saw his son and was convinced that there is life hereafter. So, this inquiring spirit comes to us and we want to know what is beyond death. The real beginning of religion is the search for the permanent Reality whom we call God, Holy One, Allah, Ahura Mazda, or Brahman.

People remain restless until they know the truth. In the *Bhagavad-Gita*, Sri Krishna says: "No knowledge (of the Self) has the unsteady. Nor has he meditation. To the unmeditative there is no peace. And how can one without peace have happiness?" (*Gita* II:66). In the *Katha Upanishad* it is said: "Neither those who have not refrained from wickedness, nor the unrestrained, nor the unmeditative, nor one with unpacified mind, can attain this (the Supreme Self) even by knowledge."[8] We do not find a single person in the world who is not seeking peace and happiness, even though he may run after what is perishable, thinking that it will make him happy. George Eastman of the Kodak Company built up a tremendous industry thinking that

---

[8] *Katha Upanishad* 11: 24.

'he would find happiness, but he ended his life by committing suicide. Innumerable persons are unhappy and miserable in their later years. Let me share one sad story of a friend who was a bank official in Providence, Rhode Island. We became friendly in 1928 and used to visit together each time he saw me in the bank. After his retirement, he lost control over his mind. When he saw me, he could only say over and over, "Oh, it is wonderful you came to see me!" Why had this happened? He had nothing to live for. Some retired men and women do not have any purpose in life because they have fixed their minds on getting something from the objective world. So when their working days are over, they lose interest in life and are frustrated. Many of them die prematurely. If they do not die, they feel perfectly miserable. There is nothing but emptiness in life for them.

One of my very good friends used to tell me how empty his life was. He had worked himself up in the textile industry from errand boy to millionaire. He had a beautiful home built after the model of an English manor with materials imported from Europe. He enjoyed high social status, was greatly respected in his church, had a wife and four children, everything that one can expect. Yet, when he was sixty years of age, he told me one day, "Swami, everything is empty." I cannot forget the look in his eyes, reflecting his agonized state of mind. Fortunately, he became interested in spiritual things two years before he died, and we used to meet frequently for spiritual discussions.

Life will remain empty unless a person seeks God. Even the process of seeking Him is gratifying. Then as one proceeds in religious practices—such as meditation, cultivation of the love of God, unselfish work, or process of analysis or reason (intellectual method), or a combination of one or more of these—a new vista opens up. The individual gets more and more satisfaction, joy, and peace. When a person reaches the goal of religion, he is full of joy. He radiates love. He does not have to argue about religion or convince himself that he must love others. He spontaneously loves everyone, just as the sun radiates light continuously. Even a questionable, demoralized person can be changed by one who has experienced God. Anyone, no matter what his qualities may be, can be changed by the highest type of spiritual person. A spiritual man or woman is able to influence others according to his own level of spiritual development. Even the sincere persons who are still struggling to live a stable and spiritual life cannot help being of service to mankind. Therefore, we need religion not only to satisfy ourselves but also to serve mankind.

Some will ask if it is not selfish to seek religion for self-satisfaction. No, it is not selfish, as the objective is to know the ultimate Reality. With that knowledge one radiates love and peace; then all persons share in this love of God, love of neighbor. The lover of God is the most unselfish person. He is the one who can truly give service to mankind. Where would we get our culture—Hindu, Jewish, Christian—or what would we attain but for these men and women established in that knowledge of God? They are the ones who lift humanity from selfish brutality to the spiritual level of life. What more can we expect of a man? We need religion in every age, for every person, in every culture. Otherwise we are bound to be demoralized, as is proved by the contemporary history of mankind. We need it for our individual peace and happiness, and for our family, national, and international peace and happiness.

WHAT IS INITIATION?

Every thinking man or woman would like to know about spiritual rebirth. Every religion advocates that a man must be reborn in order to enter the realm of God. In fact, unless one is born again in the spirit, he cannot properly comprehend God or experience Him.

Spiritual birth, or what is called initiation in India, is a very significant factor in our spiritual life. The word "initiation" has a different connotation in the West. It requires clarification, because it is used by all sorts of social and fraternal organizations in this part of the world. For instance, in the sororities and fraternities of American universities, the boys and girls receive initiation. This means that they have to dress and behave in exhibitionistic ways. Once a young student of the Massachusetts Institute of Technology was thrown into the Charles River and had to swim to the shore. Other college boys had similar experiences as part of their initiation ceremony. Initiation into religious life is quite different.

Is initiation like conversion? We often hear about conversion in the Christian tradition. However, we find that many times this conversion is of the evangelistic type. This is not true of initiation. Not long ago we were told about an evangelist who was lecturing to crowds in Boston a few years ago and informing them that there are automobiles in heaven. A man who tries to convert others with this understanding of heaven cannot really convert anyone. At the most he can put on a show or a display of emotion. This type of conversion does not mean anything at all so far as religious life is concerned. A number of years ago in Washington, D.C., a number of persons were converted, probably by the same man. A friend of mine, Dr. J. McVicker Hunt, a prominent psychologist and at present Professor in the Psychology Department in the University of Illinois, studied these conversion experiences. He followed up eleven out of twelve cases immediately after the meeting and found that they had gone back to their old ways of life the very same night. Is that real conversion? All those people were enthusiastic when the evangelist said: "Come, come, and your soul will be saved." But as soon as the meeting was over they forgot it all. Dr. Sorokin also investigated seventy-four cases of the same type of conversion, and he also found that not one man changed after that conversion experience. Is initiation this kind of conversion? Did Jesus mean this when he said we must be born again? If an individual does not change his attitudes or spiritualize his life, the conversion is meaningless.

All religions advocate conversion; but do they really expect a person to be spiritually awakened and to start a new life? We can definitely say that real conversion or initiation should open a new vista, a new way of life. Most people in the West come from the Judeo-Christian tradition. In the Jewish tradition, the *bar mitzvah* or confirmation has the same meaning that initiation has for the Hindus. In the Christian tradition, baptism or christening is used. Some Christian sects use this for small children who are later confirmed when they are more mature. In the Islamic groups there are similar practices. The Buddhists use *diksha*. This, like initiation, is meant to awaken the spiritual consciousness of the individual and give him a new start in spiritual life.

People hear and read about God; they discuss and philosophize about Him; and they indulge in theological interpretations. Still, as we all know, the lives of the people at large do not indicate that they have real understanding of God. They could not do such deplorable things if they had real spiritual understanding or a real start in spiritual life. We heard a very sad story about a religious leader who left his religious calling because of some disturbance. This would not have happened if he had developed real understanding as a spiritual teacher. Such personalities are found in every religious tradition. So conversion, initiation, or *diksha* may not always be what we expect.

Generally speaking, with a few exceptions like the above examples, it means at least a start, a new birth, a beginning in spiritual life. We may not know just what spiritual life is; but when we are initiated, we are given an introduction to it.

There are various theories given by outstanding thinkers in the Christian tradition about conversion or spiritual birth. Orthodox personalities claim that if one is not baptized one cannot go to heaven. Moreover, a person must be baptized in a particular manner. For instance, some claim that immersion is necessary; others insist that one must be sprinkled (christened) with holy water to make the ceremony valid. Also, this must be performed by an individual belonging to a particular religious group; otherwise, one cannot go to heaven or see God.

Then, again, little or no attention is given to the personal qualities of the religious teacher. So long as he belongs to a particular group, has been ordained by the proper authorities, and has been permitted to perform these ceremonies officially, then everything is all right. The level of his spiritual development is not taken into consideration. Hindus have a much different point of view. They know that the effect of initiation greatly depends on the person who gives it. If the personality of the religious teacher is not integrated, no matter how exalted his position may be in the religious institution, he cannot give the spiritual aspirant a real start in religious life. A man may go to philosophers, theologians, or the high dignitaries of a religious institution, but he cannot have spiritual awakening if he does not get initiation from a spiritually awakened individual—one who has had at least a glimpse of that Reality or God. This is the primary condition of initiation. The effect depends on both the qualities of the teacher and the qualities of the disciple.

One of the earliest psychologists of religion in this country states that conversion or rebirth can occur only when the aspirant has a sense of guilt or sin. Dr. Edwin Diller Starbuck writes: "The sense of sin and depression of feeeling are fundamental factors in conversion if not in religious experience in general."[9]

[9] Edwin Diller Starbuck, *The Psychology of Religion* (New York: Charles Scribner's Sons, 1899), pp. 58, 64, 67.

Dr. William James has a very broad viewpoint, almost similar to that of the Hindus; but he, too, gives a lingering idea of the necessity of guilt-consciousness. Dr. Walter Houston Clark says:

> Awakening may come by a gradual road. The psychologist must acknowledge two manners of spiritual growth. But the fact of the matter is that the demands of the great religions of history are so radical in their essences that no comfortable citizen can contemplate their demands without inwardly drawing back.
>
> ....
>
> This need not involve the cheap and artificial stimulation of conversion, but simply an emphasis on truth that in some personalities will lead to a transforming and creative experience of conversion.[10]

As we intimately observe the lives of persons who have been initiated, we find this guilt-consciousness or feeling of sinfulness is not necessarily a prerequisite to spiritual awakening for all individuals, but it may be present in a few. Some persons may feel inadequate. Others may feel dissatisfied because they are leading very questionable lives. For instance, St. Augustine before his conversion was leading a discouraging and sinful life. Then he became conscious of what he was doing and wanted to be reborn. Similar instances are to be found in every tradition —Hindu, Buddhistic, Jewish, and others. Again, there are others who have a sincere desire to know God, a thirst for knowledge of God, and an attraction to Him. In this group we find St. Francis of Assisi, St. Teresa of Avila, St. Thérèse of Lisieux (The Little Flower), St. John of the Cross, and such others. These persons had no feelings of guilt or sin when they turned to religion. We cannot agree with Starbuck when we study their lives. It is unlikely that St. Francis was feeling sinful when he had his wonderful spiritual experience, even though he was a soldier and had enjoyed the world as a businessman's son. Psychiatrists and psychologists try to interpret the conversion of

---

[10] Walter Houston Clark, *The Psychology of Religion* (New York: The Macmillan Co., 1958), p. 217.

St. Ignatius as motivated by love of power, claiming that when he found that he could not have a big military success, he turned to religion. There are many personalities in the Christian tradition who really wanted to know God because they were attracted to Him, and not because they felt guilty about something. John Wesley and George Fox of the English tradition, Meister Eckhart, Saint Dionysius, St. Bernard, and St. Benedict, and others like them, were drawn to God because they wanted to know Him. The most we can say is that they might have felt inadequate in this knowledge and so tried to get help; but there is no evidence that a feeling of sin or guilt was the cause for their spiritual quest.

In the Indian tradition there are innumerable persons who have sought and are seeking God even today, just to know and love Him. Let us also consider the disciples of the divine incarnations, like St. John and St. Peter, and their disciples. They were attracted to Jesus, not because of any feeling of sin, but because they were inspired by Him. The same is true of Swami Vivekananda, Swami Brahmananda, and Swami Premananda, and other disciples of Sri Ramakrishna. Swami Vivekananda asked Sri Ramakrishna, "Sir, have you seen God?" The immediate answer was, "Yes, I see Him more vividly than I see you, and you can see Him, too." I knew intimately most of the disciples of Sri Ramakrishna and their own followers and can say that all of them had the desire to know God, although a few might have had a feeling of inadequacy in the beginning of their religious life. One young man heard from a disciple of Sri Ramakrishna about various spiritual experiences and it aroused his desire to have such God-realization. The great Swami told him to go and ask Swami Brahmananda for this. Swami Brahmananda said to the young man, "For this, my child, you have to be initiated and you have to practice for a few days." The boy replied, "Yes, please give me what is needed." He wanted to experience and enjoy God. So Starbuck is not correct in saying that guilt alone is the basis of conversion. The important factor is that a person must seek God. Initiation or conversion becomes successful if he has this desire.

Initiation is the starting point for the religious life. From then on, one must grow spiritually. Now, how can an individual grow in spirituality and have experience of God? There are two factors involved: one is the contribution of the religious teacher and the other is the qualities of the student. These points have been discussed in other chapters. The teacher who gives the initiation must be established in spiritual experience. So the quality of the initiation varies with the teacher's level of development. For instance, if a person goes to an incarnation, such as Jesus or Ramakrishna, for initiation, he gets spiritual realization immediately. We have heard from the disciples of Sri Ramakrishna about their own experiences. Swami Shivananda told us one day, "We all had our *samadhi* (realization of God) during His lifetime." They were then only young boys in their teens. We know that Jesus' disciples experienced God directly. Nothing more than that is needed. The goal of spiritual life is attained with such exalted experiences.

We happen to know the details of the life of Sri Ramakrishna because we had the privilege of knowing most of His disciples. We heard from them how He would give a disciple a word to repeat, and as the word was uttered the disciple would enter a superconscious state. At another time, He would say to a disciple, "Mother, be awakened!" This happened to Swami Vivekananda, and he had the highest religious experience. In some instances, Sri Ramakrishna would write the name of God on the forehead or on the tongue with His finger, or touch the chest, and the disciples would experience God. To others He would give instructions and they would have to practice before attaining that state.

Next to the incarnations of God come the eternally free souls, as they are known by the Hindus. As we said before, they can also give such spiritual awakening, provided that they are in that high state of mind when they give the initiation. They can do it with a glance, word, or touch, the same as the incarnations.

The lesser personalities are capable of giving initiation provided that they also have spiritual experiences. However, even though these teachers are awakened souls, a person cannot have instantaneous spiritual experiences with initiation because of his own inadequacies, past tendencies, or certain predominant qualities. But if the disciple follows their advice and instructions he can reach the goal. He may be compared to the baby who has to grow a little before being able to walk. The disciple has to grow gradually to be able to walk in the field of religion. One does not meet a man like Buddha, Krishna, Jesus, or Ramakrishna in every century, so the lesser personalities must be approached. However, they must be spiritually awakened themselves. Most of the popular evangelists who go around saving the souls of the people cannot awaken spiritual consciousness. They have given no evidence of their own awakening. This may seem like a harsh statement. But Brother Lawrence could awaken spiritual consciousness, even though he held a humble position in the monastery and was not a dignitary, scholar, nor official of the church. One of the disciples of Sri Ramakrishna was a servant of a wealthy man when he first went to Him. He could never even utter the alphabet properly. But his spiritual realization was so high that he could inspire others. We had the privilege of touching his feet and sitting in his presence many times.

As we have already said, the most important requirement of a spiritual student is the sincere desire to know God. If he has that desire, the initiation is bound to be effective. Suppose that one cannot find any spiritual man to awaken in him that consciousness? What can he do? He can directly pray to God and ask that somehow he can meet a suitable person. If he is sincere and really wants to change his life, he will find help. Some who crave for an experience of God have initiation and instructions even in their dreams. We happen to know of cases in India and in this country where initiation was received from great personalities who did not exist on this plane at that time. Some psychiatrists and psychologists may say that such experiences are not from the outside or any personality; they are in the unconscious. But they cannot explain how the individual learns words (*mantras*) unknown to him or his culture in such dreams.

Suppose that a man does not even believe in God. He can

then say, as John Stuart Mill did just before his death, "If there is any God, if there is any Reality, then give me this." If the heart is panting for spiritual awakening, a person is bound to find a way. If he is earnest and sincere, God will know his heart and give help.

Suppose a person is initiated by someone who is not so religious, although he holds a place in a religious institution. Even then, if the person is really initiated and if he really is sincere, that initiation will become operative, because God knows the heart and its hankering. In a mysterious way, He will utilize the initiation and lift the person to a higher plane.

Then there is the question of Judas. He was a disciple of Jesus, so why would he betray Him? Or we could ask the same question about some of the disciples of other great personalities. Why do we find such disturbing and changeable elements in them? The answer is that some disciples have such strong unconscious drives and urges on the lower plane of existence that they cannot perceive the Truth or Reality at that time. However, the effect of the initiation remains in them. As soon as the unconscious drives and urges wear out—either through satisfaction, reasoning, or right spiritual practices—then the effect will become visible. They are bound to change. Sooner or later the old *samskaras* (unconscious impressions and urges) wear out.

Many persons cannot give up their childhood experiences. Even though they become old, they still cling to their old reactions and do not want to forget their unpleasant experiences with their mother, father, brother, or step-mother and the like. However, even these reactions will change in time if the disciple is sincere and persistent in following the instructions of his spiritual teacher. Then the disciple grows in spiritual experience and realization. Then alone can he say, "Yes, there is a God, because I see Him; I experience Him."

5

SPIRITUAL METHODS

Preparation for the fulfillment of spiritual ideals is definitely required of an individual. Many persons think that they have understanding of the glories of spiritual life because they have read certain books or have experienced a surge of emotional or poetical or philosophical flight. It is quite possible that they have attained intellectual understanding; but if anyone wants to have real fulfillment in spiritual life, he must prepare himself for it.

In certain religious groups some thinkers conclude that only faith in God or an historical personality like Jesus is needed. According to them this is the whole meaning of religion. Some go so far as to say only those religions are valid which depend entirely on faith. They claim that this faith should transform the personality and should enable people to live the life that Jesus advocated and to fulfill the Sermon on the Mount and the second commandment of Jesus: "Love thy neighbor." Historical evidences from an earlier period of this century, described by Dr. Pitirim Sorokin, Dr. Howard Mumford Jones, and Dr. Oswald Spengler, prove that the claims about faith made in religious life are in error. In fact, this is also substantiated by evidence from contemporary history during the last two World Wars and the present incidents occurring in Africa and the southern part of the United States. No individual should be blamed for failure to carry out the ideal as taught by Jesus and other valid authorities, like the great mystics from Christianity, Judaism, Hinduism, Islam, Buddhism, and Taoism. It can only be said that mere scriptural study or acceptance of scriptures, doctrines, and dogmas, and faith in their validity, do not change the personality. If one does not work for expression of the ideals taught by the great spiritual personalities, he will act with bigotry, prejudice, and so on. These are, unfortunately, human weaknesses. So we learn a great lesson from destructive historical events, that preparation and training are absolutely necessary for the attainment of the goal of religion.

We also know, from an academic point of view, that a man cannot become a real philosopher or a real scientist without training. Einstein, Eddington, or Shapley did not become great scientists accidentally. They did not produce such wonderful work with only their faith in the possibility of human achievement. Philosophers like Socrates, Plato, Plotinus, Philo, Maimonides, Kant, Hegel, and others in the West did not become philosophers accidentally. Of course, the religious groups who claim that religion is nothing but faith may say that there is no relationship between the attainment of the scholars and the attainment of religious people.

Some of them also claim that in the "utter agony" and awareness of the sinful state of man, complete surrender to the historical personality of Jesus is necessary so that He will redeem us. According to them, religious experience or revelation comes from God, from above. Human beings cannot do anything more than to surrender themselves. We admit that there have been a few historical personalities, both in the Orient and the Occident, who had spiritual revelation or mystic experience almost accidentally, it seems. Some of them, like St. Paul, St. Augustine, and St. Francis, did not have to suffer "utter agony," but had spontaneous spiritual revelation. However, most of the great spiritual personalities belonging to the various religions experienced God after following certain training processes.

That is the very reason Cabalistic and Hasidic Jews prescribe certain types of religious practices, as do Christian mystics from the Apostles of Jesus to the present, including St. Francis, St. Ignatius, St. Teresa of Avila, St. John of the Cross, George Fox, and John Wesley. The same is true of the Islamic tradition and the Hindu, Buddhistic, and Taoist traditions. We find that they have thoroughgoing scientific methods for verifying the existence of God, which are just as good as those of any other religious groups. It is understood and declared by the great personalities of all these religious traditions that any one who goes

63

through a process of training and spiritual practices can have valid spiritual experiences.

The grace of God is an important factor in spiritual life. But the seekers of truth must make an effort, or they will not be able to utilize God's grace. Sri Ramakrishna used to say that if you go one step toward God, he comes three steps toward you. So a little effort is required in the form of spiritual practices. Those who only talk about grace or faith do not show any change in their lives or personalities. We witnessed during the last two World Wars that many religious leaders in the West advocated destructive activities.[11]

If the inner temple of a man's being is polluted, he cannot reach the heights of spiritual glory, attainable only when the inner temple is completely pure and fit for the glorification of that ideal. Thus it is essential for that person to be established in ethical principles. The cultivation of ethics is the primary stage of spiritual practices. Patanjali, the father of Hindu psychology, said that without this a man cannot go through higher spiritual practices. It must be remembered that ethical living is not the end or the goal of religion. It comes rather at the beginning of spiritual life, and becomes gradually a spontaneous function. One of the most important reasons for ethical culture is that it stabilizes the mind by eliminating disturbing drives and urges, while it reconstructs the beneficial, harmonious, and peaceful mental tendencies.

The spiritual goal can be reached individually, not collectively. Only divine incarnations or great spiritual personalities, known in India as eternally free souls, have the power to lift a multitude to a higher plane of consciousness. We have seen this happen when disciples of Sri Ramakrishna lifted whole groups to the highest state of consciousness, even those with questionable characters. Such people were transported to another plane of consciousness so that they temporarily forgot where they were. However, they could not retain that exalted state without spiritual practices.

---

[11] Karl Barth, *This Christian Cause* (New York: The Macmillan Co., 1941), chap. 1.

When we were with Swami Brahmananda in Calcutta serving him, a prominent doctor went to the monastery and knelt before him. Since we were present and stood behind Swami Brahmananda fanning him, we witnessed this scene. The doctor saluted the great Swami in Indian fashion by touching his feet with his head. With feeling he said, "Give me something." He meant realization of God rather than something material. Swami Brahmananda smiled a little and replied, "You know, through the Master's grace we can lift you but we cannot take you down." Then he joked with the doctor, saying, "You have your family and children. Who will take care of them if you get intoxicated?" Finally he became serious. "Wait a little while," he told this man. During the latter period of his life, the doctor devoted his whole life to spiritual realization and the service of man. Swami Brahmananda used to tell us, "Yes, we can lift you up, but you have to retain that state." The power of retention can be had only when a person has prepared himself through spiritual exercises.

The multitude was transported by Jesus. Yet, those very persons went against him because they did not have the power to retain the spiritual exaltation. Every man must individually develop the power of retention. Even though the spiritual realization may be given to a person and he is lifted to a higher plane of existence, he must be established in his practices and be purified enough to make these experiences his own.

Even though they did not need to do so, the incarnations went through spiritual practices. Buddha, Jesus, and Sri Ramakrishna were always conscious of their true nature. Ordinary men and women do not have this awareness. But with preparation, training, and discipline, they can become God-conscious. The incarnations went through spiritual discipline and training to show others that it is necessary and to teach them the various methods which should be and can be used by different individuals, according to their inner requirements. When we study the life of Sri Ramakrishna, we find that he took up different methods at different times. It is very important that a person use a method suitable to his own temperament rather than imitate another, even if he has a close and intimate relationship with another as friend, husband or wife, parent or child, and so on, no matter how sweet and loving the relationship may be.

Spiritual realization is generally not superimposed, except in special instances by divine incarnations or other great spiritual personalities. Spiritual realization comes ordinarily from an evolutionary process, after an individual has gone through spiritual practices suitable to him. These practices are known in India as *yogas*. The word yoga literally means method of attaining union with God. It is often misrepresented in the West as a method of extrasensory perception and control of the laws of nature. The *yogas* are classified into four groups. There are also subdivisions of these groups, which will not be discussed here. These methods are used for inner or mental purification and stability through discrimination, work, meditation, or devotion and love.

The money exchangers of the Jewish people, at the time of Jesus, polluted the temple because they took gross desires of enjoyment into the temple activities. The same is true today. The hedonistic pleasure principle is constantly polluting the mentality of the people and diluting their ideals. First, they try to rationalize pleasure, then they dilute the spiritual ideal to fit into the scheme of life. With this search for enjoyment, power, and so on, certain inner and outer conflicts are created. Psychologically speaking, as long as there are mental conflicts there is no possibility of inner peace and stability. It is said in the *Bhagavad-Gita*:

> No knowledge (of the Self) has the unsteady. Nor has he meditation. To the unmeditative there is no peace. And how can one without peace have happiness?
>
> For the mind which follows in the wake of the wandering senses, carries away his discrimination, as a wind (carries away from its course) a boat on the waters.[12]

The same idea is given in the Upanishads.

---

[12] *Srimad-Bhagavad-Gita*, trans. Swami Swarupananda (Mayavati, Almora, Himalayas: Advaita Ashrama, 1933), II: 66-67.

Are the urges and desires for pleasure to be repressed? V. all know that it is not good to repress these tendencies, as neurotic conditions and functional ailments are created. Some of the modern psychologists and psychiatrists say that these tendencies should be expressed; then peace of mind is attained. However, the cultivation of discrimination is needed in the expression of the so-called natural propensities and urges, for they are intensified with uncontrolled expressions and require more and more outlet. The results are then disastrous. People do have a higher nature with certain religious ideals and ideas, along with what Thomas à Kempis calls "inordinate affections" and what many psychiatrists term "natural drives." No matter how people may try to repress them, these drives come to the surface. When they are expressed without any higher understanding or discipline they become diabolical instincts. Then comes the conflict between the higher and lower nature. No religious man would advocate a method of repression or inhibition. Jesus, Ramakrishna, and other such personalities advocate understanding, control, discipline, and proper use of these so-called natural tendencies.

For proper understanding of his inner nature, natural tendencies, and higher ideals, an intellectual man follows the method of discrimination by use of his intellect, or the path of *Jnana Yoga*. He must cultivate the six treasures or jewels of spiritual life: external and internal self-control, patience, endurance, purity, faith in one's self and God, meditation and other such spiritual exercises. When one cultivates these qualities, then alone is one fit to think of the Absolute. A man ought to use discrimination. Thereby he finds what is abiding joy and what is relative joy, what is permanent and what is temporary. He struggles to overcome the opposite and to become established in the permanent and abiding. In this way the intellectual individual cleanses his inner nature. The moment the inner nature is purified, the truth reveals itself. Man realizes the unity of God and soul.

Buddha declared: "The fourth noble truth is the eightfold

o the cessation of sorrow."[13] The eightfold path
1) right understanding, (2) right aspiration, (3)
(4) right conduct, (5) right mode of livelihood,
ort, (7) right meditation, (8) right realization.
of living, which includes discrimination, can lead
anyone to the highest truth. In the Buddhistic tradition many
persons followed the path of knowledge throughout the centuries. Through right understanding and meditation they
reached the highest truth.

A second method, followed by the active person, is called
Karma Yoga. This individual does unselfish work. He performs
his duties in the spirit of service, consecration, and worship. We
observe that every man works with a motive, whether it is for
money, power, position, recognition, and so on. Do we not observe men and women who are successful because they systematically and thoroughly devote their time and energy to these
objectives? On the other hand, a spiritual aspirant succeeds also
if he can keep up his spirit of service and worship. His objective
is different; it is the realization of God. Consequently, he tenaciously concentrates on this goal in and through his work and
service. By doing so he attains inner purification and expands
his consciousness. He finds the expression of the Self in all. He
spontaneously overcomes envy, jealousy, greed, anger, pride,
and love of power. It would seem that such a man is not going
through any particular practice or worship. Nevertheless, if he
persists in the service of God and the service of man with right
understanding, without caring for external results, he will grow
spiritually. If he practices the presence of God in the midst of
his activities, whatever they may be, he can reach the ultimate
goal. In the Christian tradition, Brother Lawrence and such
other personalities among Catholics and Protestants demonstrate the validity of *Karma Yoga*. Through good works, the
inner temple becomes pure and fit for the advent of God.

In *Karma Yoga* it is not the type of work that matters but the

---

[13] Paul Carus, *The Gospel of Buddha* (Chicago: The Open Court Publish-
ing Co., 1894), XII: 11-14.

attitude toward it. In the history of mankind we find many persons who realized God by performing their respective duties. In the Indian tradition a king named Janaka reached the highest spiritual realization by performing his duties as a ruler, according to the manner described in the *Bhagavad-Gita*.[14] There is a very interesting episode related in Hindu religious literature. A young boy left his home to become an itinerant monk, begging food from house to house and intensifying his spiritual practices. One day he sat under a tree meditating. The birds were flying around, dropping leaves on him, and making rustling sounds. The young man felt annoyed because of the disturbance and he looked at the birds with such anger that he killed them with his glance. When it was time for him to eat, he went to a neighborhood village to beg for food. According to the orthodox custom of an itinerant monk, he stood in front of a house and called the name of God three times. It is the usual custom that if there is no response the monk should move on to another house. Just as he was about to go away, a feeble voice was heard from inside the house where he was standing: "My son, do not be annoyed. My husband is sick and I am taking care of him. After that I shall come and give you food. I am not like the birds, so please do not be annoyed." The young fellow was then startled and wondered how this lady could know what had happened in the morning of that day. So he waited. After a little while she brought some food to the door and gave it to him in a motherly way. The boy asked her: "How did you know that I killed the birds with my anger?" She replied: "By performing my duty as a housewife, I developed certain spiritual understanding. If you want to know more about this, go to the village market where you will find a butcher. He can give you the highest truth." With great curiosity he went to the butcher who saw him approaching from a distance and recognized his spirit of inquiry. "My child," he told the young man, "I shall talk with you after I finish my work and take care of my old father." The young man waited patiently. Finally, the but-

---

[14] *Srimad-Bhagavad-Gita*, chap. III.

cher returned to him and started to talk about the Absolute. He was on a high level of consciousness. He had reached the state of highest spiritual realization by performing his duties as a butcher and as a son. Similar instances are to be found in the Indian tradition. Such cases must be known in other religious traditions. So we find that an individual can realize the highest truth by performing his duties without attachment to them, in the spirit of service and dedication.

Those who have a basic devotional nature and take God as a personal Being with qualities, attributes, name, and form should think of serving God through His children. They are to try to feel the presence of their chosen ideal—Jesus, or Buddha, Krishna, Ramakrishna, or such other personified aspect of God —in members of their family, co-workers, colleagues, and others. They should dedicate the results of their work to the personal God.

There are some who adopt the impersonal aspect of God as their ideal. These people must cultivate the idea that everyone is the manifestation of the Ultimate Reality. When they serve others in any way they should try to feel the presence of the Absolute in them and perform the service without attachment.

The agnostics and skeptics, who cannot use either of the two above attitudes, should work for others without attachment or caring for the results or for what they can get out of it. It is important that they try to eliminate egocentricity, self-centeredness, and selfish gratification in the performance of action. Agnostics or skeptics or even atheists can reach the highest truth by following this method of *Karma Yoga*, although they may start their spiritual life without accepting the existence of God, personal or impersonal.

The third method is known as the path of meditation, or *Raja Yoga*. A meditative person concentrates his mind on an aspect or a symbol of God. In the course of his regular meditation he removes all his inordinate tendencies. This is possible because he, at least temporarily, withdraws his mind from the outer objects of sensation and the inner unconscious drives and urges, accumulated by positive or negative past experiences and by so-called repressions. When an individual withdraws his mind from the objective world during meditation, he overcomes the effects of the objective world which disturb the mind and create hatred, jealousy, love of power. Even though he may sit for meditation for only a few minutes in the morning and evening, at that time he withdraws his mind from the objects which stimulate lower passions. The result is that the lower passions do not have a hold on him any more. His mind becomes pure. This struggle to concentrate on one aspect of God manifests inner power of the mind. The result is mental integration, even though it may be only temporary at first. Then as the person progresses, the mind becomes wholly unified, while the lower impressions and tendencies drop off.

This is not repression. It is rather a process of rebuilding or re-education, as some of the outstanding psychiatrists and psychologists like Dr. Karen Horney and Dr. Hobart Mowrer say. By this method the unconscious mind is rebuilt with constructive, positive, and dynamic ideas and feelings, without any negation or pessimism. Sri Ramakrishna used to say, "The more you go toward Benares, the farther away remains Calcutta." This method of meditation is like travelling the road to a destination away from internal and external disturbances. The mind becomes filled with dynamic power in the thought of God.

There are some among religious groups who are afraid of meditation. They say that prayer is sufficient. Little do they understand that real prayer is not possible so long as the mind remains disturbed and full of conflict and turmoil, even though the words of the prayer may be uttered in a formal way. Prayer cannot be effective if one's thoughts are wandering everywhere. Only when the mind is trained to be one-pointed and concentrated through the practice of meditation on God will prayer be effective.

There are critics who say that meditation is withdrawal of the mind from the realities of life. This is a mistaken idea. It is true that in meditation the mind is withdrawn for the time being from the objective world. However, at the same time, the mind is focused on what is really real, namely, the Absolute or

7 1

God. This is not a negative mental state. On the contrary, it is dynamic and positive even in the earlier stages of practice. As a person progresses, his latent powers become manifested. It can be compared to the rays of the sun which give intense heat and light when converged. So it is with the mind. When it is withdrawn from the objects of sense perception it is focused on the Reality or God. As a result, its potential powers become dynamic, creative, and illumining.

Those who are by nature emotional take a personified aspect of God—such as Jesus, Krishna, Buddha, Ramakrishna, and such other personalities—and concentrate the mind on the personality of their choice. The majority of the people need a picture or a statue to concentrate the mind. One has to form the habit of visualizing that form, forgetting all other thought. It requires tremendous patience and perseverance to train this restless mind to remain focused on this.

Others, predominantly intellectual by nature, cannot focus on a personification of God or a picture or a statue. They are asked to concentrate their mind on light as a symbol which signifies the universal qualities of the Absolute, or on other universal symbols prescribed by the different religious traditions. Again, there are persons who find it very difficult to visualize a symbol. Hindus advise them to focus their minds on a distant sound as it is heard on the seashore or in a deep forest. However, any of these methods of concentration requires time. We have to be extremely patient with ourselves and persevere for some time. Then alone the mind gets settled.

The question may arise: Why should one use a personal aspect of God or a symbol of the Absolute? The reason for this is that, generally speaking, the mind is incapable of thinking of anything beyond name, form, qualities, attributes. The Absolute cannot be the object of thought. Meditation is concentrated thought of an aspect or symbol of God, negating all other thoughts which are based on ordinary and usual experiences. So it is necessary for the majority of the people to follow one of these two methods in meditation for real illumination and integration of emotions and manifestation of dynamic hidden power of mind.

There are persons who cannot think of any aspect or personification or symbol of God. They may be agnostics, atheists, or even materialists. They are advised by Hindus and Buddhists to empty the mind of all thoughts and leave it vacant. This is the most difficult method of concentration and meditation, as everyone is in the habit of thinking continually of something. The moment the mind is emptied and withdrawn from usual experiences, the unconscious drives and urges rise to the surface and keep the mind preoccupied. So this method is difficult for the vast majority of people. There is also a danger that the mind will become passive and negative unless the person is trained by a competent teacher and the student proceeds with great care. Therefore, the two methods of devotion and meditation on a symbol of the Absolute are more highly advocated.

The fourth and most natural of all methods is *Bhakti Yoga*. It is, therefore, applicable to the greatest number of people. Sri Ramakrishna describes it:

> There is, however, another path leading to God—the path of devotion (Bhakti Yoga). If once man gains love of God, if once the chanting of His holy "name" begins to thrill the devotee with joy, what effort is needed for the control of passions afterwards? The control comes of itself.[15]

Almost all persons are basically emotional. Even most of those who talk about philosophy and rationalism are primarily emotional. It is amazing to know that in spite of philosophical discussions, a little change in the environment or some emotional reaction can seriously affect the individuals involved. At that time philosophy has no place in their lives. They react just as any person in that state of mind would do. So intellectualism is, after all, nothing but a veneer for most people. There are only a few exceptional individuals who can practice the intel-

---

[15] *Sayings of Sri Ramakrishna* (7th revised ed.; Mylapore, Madras: Sri Ramakrishna Math, 1949), XVI: 751.

lectual method. As the devotional method is applicable to the vast majority of people, we shall elaborate on it here.

In *Bhakti Yoga*, the emotions are used for the realization of God. These emotions are the most powerful implements, the most powerful drives found in human beings. So, instead of crushing them, the Hindu teachers advocate that they be cultivated and redirected to God. Sri Ramakrishna used to say that the emotions are not bad at all, that they should be used in spiritual practices. We remember one young man who approached Swami Brahmananda one day complaining that he was very emotional. Swami Brahmananda understood and consoled him, saying, "My child, who is not emotional? Emotions are not bad. But one has to use a little discrimination." Almost everyone has strong and ardent emotions of one type or another. People have problems when they misuse or misdirect them.

Various emotions are found among the devotees. Some have attachment for the mother or the father, others for the child. In some instances, conjugal love is the most attractive. For some, the friend is the most loved. Such emotions can be directed to God, the devotee regarding Him as parent, child, spouse, or friend, whichever is most suitable. When the emotional relationship is achieved it is called *bhava*, a relationship of intense love.

Most people are not aware of the various ways in which one can love God. They are taught that there is only one way to reach Him. A number of years ago an elderly lady attended one of our services. Later she told a friend, "The Swami talked so nicely, but he did not say anything about God." The term "Father in Heaven" had not been used! God is called by various names; but certain names are taught in particular religions. So the people feel that a person using any other name is not worshipping God. This narrow attitude does not help anyone. In fact, it has created serious disturbances in the minds of the people in Europe and America, actually driving many away from the threshold of religion.

No matter what relationship an individual establishes, he must follow it systematically according to his own inherent tendencies. All emotions, all thoughts must be directed to God through this relationship. In studying the life of Sri Ramakrishna, we find that He first followed what is called the natural method. He did not go through any discipline or prescribed series of practices. His heart was panting for the realization of God. He knew God was the Mother of the universe in the temple where He was living. He wanted to experience Her. This desire was so intense that it consumed Him. The Mother of the universe could not help but reveal Herself to Him, as we know from His life.

Then a great woman of renunciation and high spiritual realization went to the temple and taught Him different methods for realizing God, practiced by a particular religious philosophy or school of thought in India. Under her tutelage, Sri Ramakrishna reached the same state of God-consciousness through each method after a very short time. So He found that God could be reached through all the various methods.

He was not one-sided in His spiritual relationship with God. After finding God as the Mother, He took God as His son and child. Just as a mother trains and disciplines a son and loves him, so Sri Ramakrishna saw God as an infant and found perfection in the expression of that emotion, in exalted spiritual realization.

Then again, He worshipped God as Master and associated Himself as the servant. He followed that system in such a way that His very physical structure was changed. It is amazing how thoughts can change the physical condition of a man according to the ideal he follows. Sri Ramakrishna reached the highest state of consciousness by following this method and establishing the relationship of Master and servant, Lord and devotee. He also established friendship with God.

When we study the lives of saints in Christianity and other religions, we find that every one of them had his or her own relationship with God. St. Anthony of Padua, St. Maria of Genoa, St. Francis, St. Clara, St. Teresa of Avila, St. John of the Cross, Rabbi Israel (Baal Shem) and others had a definite loving relationship. In Sri Ramakrishna's life we find that He adopted different relationships at different times to prove the validity of all of them. He demonstrated empirically to the contemporary world that valid methods practiced by different spiritual personalities in their emotional relationships with God are equally effective and powerful. The world needed this validation, and He fulfilled this great need.

Then He followed a method which does not require an emotional relationship. In this path, *Jnana Yoga*, He established oneness of God and soul. After having verified the various Hindu methods, He followed practices in Christianity, Islam, and Buddhism, and reached the same state of God-consciousness in all of them. Incarnations of God have a definite purpose in whatever they do. In taking up the various methods in the different religions, Sri Ramakrishna demonstrated to the world that every one of them would lead to the highest state of God-consciousness.

Let not anyone think that his own method is the best. The emotional method is best for the emotional person, just as the intellectual method is best for the intellectual person. Let not anyone imitate another in his attitude or relationship with God. It is most important that a spiritual aspirant take up a method which is easiest and most suited to him and then follow it faithfully. One must be thorough in his practices.

When Sri Ramakrishna followed the Hindu, Christian, Islamic, or Buddhistic methods, He strictly followed the customs and traditions of those religions. He did not mix two systems. From His glorious personality we learn that one must be thorough in spiritual practices. When a person really wants inner purification through any one of these methods, he will establish harmonious living and a peaceful state of mind, and God will reveal Himself.

So long as a man keeps his mind full of impurities, such as Jesus found in the vendors of the temple, there is no possibility of higher realization. Let not the inner temple of man be polluted by materialistic desires and the pleasure principle. We cannot enjoy God and at the same time cling to hatred, envy, jealousy, and greed. People are often disturbed by these tendencies but they generally place the blame for them on others.

However, they are envious, jealous, and so on only because of their inner impurities.

There are individuals who combine two or more of the four methods: *Jnana Yoga, Karma Yoga, Raja Yoga,* and *Bhakti Yoga.* For instance, a man may have an intellectual background and culture and discrimination. At the same time he performs his work in the spirit of service and dedication. He also tries to maintain an emotional relationship with God; and he practices concentration and meditation. Those who practice the four methods more or less together have a harmonious development of all functions of the mind. We have to admit that such persons are few and far between. Swami Vivekananda declared that those who follow a combination of the four methods develop into ideal persons. This is not to be mistaken for eclecticism; it is rather a harmonizing of the four paths. Is the realization of God an outcome of the particular method? Or to put the question another way: Does the method itself determine the spiritual realization? The answer is, no. Spiritual practices or methods are the conditions of God-realization. They do not create it. They prepare the individual for the realization of what is already inherent in man. Spiritual practices make the manifestation of divine knowledge possible; they remove the obstacles. The moment these obstacles, the inordinate tendencies, are removed, the light shines through and a person experiences spontaneous revelation or knowledge of God. That is the reason the early Buddhists emphasized the Fourth Truth, namely, right living, right meditation, and so on. Even now, there are some schools of Buddhism which still follow the method of *Dhyana,* meditation. Their purpose is to make the mind one-pointed and free from impurities and restlessness. Then, as Buddha declared, the Truth reveals itself. In all of this, the grace of God has a very important place, as we have said earlier in this chapter.

There are some auxiliary methods to help us so that we can really concentrate our mind on the personality of God or a symbol of God. The collective service or worship conducted by different religions is helpful for that purpose. In some traditions of orthodox Christianity, they conduct the mass. Thereby they try to cultivate the thought of the personality of Jesus. Other traditions like Jewish, Protestant Christian and Muslim have their worship services in different ways. Nevertheless they are also helpful in the earlier stage of spiritual development. Similarly, Hindus and Buddhists have their collective rituals to fulfill this purpose.

We are also taught to cultivate the spirit of worship individually. There are two types of worship, external worship and internal worship. In external worship, different ingredients are used: flowers, incense, perfume, water, food, light, and so forth. Through these offerings we are to think of a particular aspect of God to whom we offer these. This individual or personal worship is very helpful for the practice of concentration as well as for the cultivation of love.

In internal worship we are trained to offer the ingredients of our body and mind and our tendencies of love, patience, forgiveness, endurance, sympathy, and such other qualities. In internal worship we do not take anything external, but we only use our imaginative faculty and thereby cultivate the thought of God. These two forms of worship are used to cultivate the thought of God. This thought gradually creates attraction. Then we fall in love and finally this love makes us realize God. The great Christian, Jewish, Hindu, and Sufi Islamic mystics all cultivated love in various ways, as we have already explained.

We are advised to remember Him in and through our activities. This remembrance helps us to cultivate the service motive and also to unify the mind.

Scriptural studies are also helpful. They remind us of the objective of life and also how to reach the objective. This frequent reminding gradually stabilizes our mind. Scriptural study is advocated by all religions. Its real purpose is to remind us of the goal of life.

Spiritual conversations or lectures are also regarded as auxiliary methods. It is true that different persons will have to take different auxiliary methods according to their own individual predispositions. It is a mistake to think that a particular method is the only method to help us to cultivate the love and thought of God. Every individual has to take up the auxiliary methods according to his or her own inherent tendencies. Otherwise if they are forced on anyone, he is likely to rebel and to develop a kind of distaste not only for auxiliary methods but also for religion. Religious teachers, as we explained before, should take up the persuasive method with sympathy and love. Then alone, the people are willing to follow religious practices.

6

THE PSYCHOLOGICAL ASPECTS OF
RELIGIOUS SYMBOLS

Many religions are criticized as superstitious and idolatrous. It is true that primitive religions have many unfamiliar customs. We often hear in the West that the Oriental religions, especially Hinduism and Buddhism, are idolatrous. This is largely due to the misunderstanding and misinterpretation of the use of symbols. It is also interesting to note that some religions use one kind of symbols while others use another kind. Yet one group criticizes the other and condemns it as idolatrous because the symbols are not identical. It is unfortunate that dogmatic persons among the different religions condemn the use of symbols, even though they have their own symbols, pictures, statues, or various other forms.

Let us consider the use of symbols in religion. The question arises: Is the use of symbols necessary? Herein lies the utility of a clear understanding of the meaning of religion. Without a proper understanding of the significance and goal of religion, we cannot understand the psychological aspects of religious symbols. So we must be dispassionate, open-minded, and thoroughly objective. Also, in this age of science, the religious leaders should remember that the meaning and use of symbols must be presented within their proper environmental and psychological background.

We admit there are many persons even in this modern age who seek religion to get power, position, health, wealth, even victory in war. During the last two world wars many religious leaders sought victory instead of peace. However, there were some who sought peace through religious observances. According to the Hindu viewpoint, there are four types of persons who seek religion and go through spiritual practices with various motives. These motives are prevalent in all religious groups.

In the age of science, the attitude of those who want to know God and have knowledge of the Reality is not only to experience God but also to convince rationalistic and scientific thinkers of the validity of spiritual knowledge through direct experience. To be a real seeker of truth, a scientist must look for the facts without preconceived notions and prejudices.

There are different types of persons among those who want knowledge of the Reality. Some are interested in verifying the existence of God for their own knowledge and to have more and more realization of His true nature. Others are not merely satisfied with the knowledge of God through direct experience, but they also want to love Him and see His presence in others and love them. Of course, there are scientifically developed persons whose attitude is actually to verify spiritual truths and share them with others.

As far as religious experiences are concerned, the seekers of God are not satisfied with mere theories, doctrines, or "faith." They want verification of the existence of the Ultimate Reality or God. They are not interested in what they can get out of God. They want to know His nature.

The first two groups naturally seek the personal aspect of God. When the Reality is personified it must be associated with name, form, qualities, and attributes. These people have to use the personified aspect of God through the use of symbols, statues, and pictures in order to think of a person with name and form to whom they can pray. The moment they personify the Absolute, that very moment, out of psychological necessity, they have to use symbols to signify the required qualities. So we find that almost all religious groups have symbols, although they are different. However, this does not mean that one symbol is valid while the other is not. The Absolute can be apprehended in different ways by different types of minds. Nevertheless, all these are ways to the Absolute, if they are sincerely followed. Therefore, the objective observer should always understand the necessity for various types of symbols for those of different cultural backgrounds. Every religious culture has its own particular symbolism which is just as valid as any other. Sri Ramakrishna says, "God is one, but His aspects are many. God is described in various ways, according to the particular aspect in which He appears to His particular worshipper."[16]

The seekers of truth and knowledge of God also have to use symbols and substitutes in the form of pictures and statues out of psychological necessity. Many of them may not be interested in gifts and blessings, as their interest is mainly to know and experience the Reality or God. Others are not merely interested in knowing God empirically, as they want to have a loving relationship with God. They want to experience Him and love Him. It is easy to say, "Love God," but in order to attain that experience He must be known and He must be a personal Being. One cannot love an impersonal Being who is beyond time, space, name, and form.

There was a very interesting incident which took place some time ago which illustrates that without experience of God we cannot love Him; nor can we depend on Him or surrender ourselves to Him in the manner that many modern theologians understand surrender. A young mother gave her little boy his supper one night and took him to his room to put him to bed. When he was in bed she kissed him goodnight, put out the light, and closed the door. The little boy began to cry. The mother opened the door and inquired, "Why are you crying?" He replied, "I am alone in the dark." Then the mother said, "God is with you." But the child told her, "I don't see God." He could depend on his mother but not on God, for he could not see God. The same is true of everyone else. Actual experience of God is required in order that we may surrender ourselves to Him. It is very easy to say that we surrender ourselves to God; but have we really done it? If a man has surrendered himself to God, he cannot write a letter like the one Karl Barth wrote to Churchill, called *This Christian Cause*.[17] "The Churches ought today to pray in all penitence and sobriety to bear witness to

[16] *Ibid.*, XI: 477.
[17] Barth, chap. I.

all the world that it is necessary and worth while to fight and to suffer for this *just peace*." Nor can we support what was advocated by Reinhold Niebuhr during the Second World War.[18] It is a philosophy of defeatists who feel utterly incompetent to follow the teachings of Christ yet who want to justify nonreligious tendencies in terms of Christian ideology. A man who experiences God is free from ego. At that time real surrender comes, as occurred in the life of great mystics like St. Francis and others in the Christian tradition, and such other personalities in the Jewish, Buddhist, Hindu, and Islamic traditions.

We find there are two classes of people in the third and fourth groups of religious seekers, those who want knowledge of God: the devotional and the intellectual. It is true that they all want to have valid religious experiences, directly and immediately, yet they vary in their conception of God. Religious persons of the devotional type necessarily have to use symbols to signify the personality of God. One cannot love, really and truly, unless there is personality. So personality must be taken in the form of a symbol to signify the qualities that are associated with God. At their present state of religious evolution, most of the people have to think in terms of personality represented by symbols. It is a psychological necessity that different religious groups, even though mature, use symbols to help the minds of the devotees to think of God and to move step by step toward spiritual realization.

The cultivation of love in religion is the opposite of the cultivation of human love. In ordinary life, we see a person, fall in love with him, and then we think of him. In religious life, it is the reverse. We think of God, fall in love with Him, and then we experience Him. That is the reason, from a psychological point of view, that we cannot think of anything which has no personification and which is beyond name and form.

This reminds me of an incident in my life which shows how the Hindu philosophers are wise and have penetrating understanding of the human mind. Just before I came to this country

---

[18] Reinhold Niebuhr, *Christianity and Power Politics* (New York: Charles Scribner's Sons, 1940).

in 1926, a friend of mine who was a monk of our order and formerly a doctor took me to visit his professor, who was also an outstanding doctor and philosopher. When we met, we began to discuss the Absolute and knowledge of the Absolute. I mentioned that one must meditate on It, and I used the Hindu term *Brahman*. A gentleman in very humble clothes was sitting in the corner of the room listening to our conversation. The moment I said that one must meditate on the Absolute, this gentleman asked, "What did you say?" I realized my inadequacy immediately and said, "Qualified Absolute," meaning Absolute with qualities, attributes, name, and form. He remained silent then. He was one of the greatest philosophers of Indian thought at that time. This brings out the fact that our finite minds, as they are at present, cannot comprehend the Absolute until the mind is developed. So we need a symbol or personification of the Absolute in order to train the mind. Then we can go beyond the limitations of the categories of knowledge. Until one reaches what the Hindus call *samadhi*, or what Professor James calls the superconscious, we must use symbols or substitutes suitable to one's personality and stage of spiritual growth. This is not idolatry or superstition. That is also the reason that different religions give different symbols so that the thought of God can be cultivated. Generally, without the thought of God there is no possibility of religious experience. The various religions use different symbols to suit the particular mental constitution of the individuals. Cultural traditions influence considerably the choice of symbols. Therefore, it is easier for spiritual aspirants to think of God if the symbols are consistent both with their mental constitutions and cultural backgrounds. It is essential that the symbols be selected on this basis; otherwise the use of symbols will not be effective and may actually obstruct the cultivation of spiritual love. It is absolutely wrong to force one type of symbol on a person if it is not suitable to him. Psychological adaptability in the use of symbols in religion is extremely important.

It should be noted here that in order to cultivate love of God, to manifest higher qualities of patience, forgiveness, sympathy, and to conquer hatred, envy, jealousy, and such other inordinate tendencies, one must intensify spiritual practices so that the mind may be unified and integrated. The positive aspect of religion is the cultivation of higher qualities and the conquest of destructive tendencies. Unless we do it, we cannot have any love for God. We are in a peculiar predicament, for in order to know the Reality, the devotional type of seekers must cultivate love. Consequently, they must have a symbol or personification of the Absolute to think of Him and cultivate that love. Without the use of symbols and personifications the devotional type of persons among the seekers of God cannot really grow. It is a psychological problem and it has to be faced from a psychological point of view. Many religious leaders may not rationally present the necessity for the use of symbols with a psychological emphasis; however, from observation of the great spiritual personalities of the world and the seekers of truth in different ages and cultures, we are compelled to accept the fact that symbols are a psychological necessity for religious growth and spiritual knowledge.

Let us consider the Christian conception of the Trinity. Here we find the personification of the Absolute in the form of Son of God, divine incarnation, Jesus. The three aspects are of the same Absolute. Yet Jesus indicated that we cannot reach God the Father without God the Son and God the Holy Spirit. There is nothing wrong in personification of the Absolute. In fact, it is necessary from a psychological point of view, in order to establish a relationship and thereby cultivate one-pointed love for Him. Historically it has been found that people who have dynamic relationships with the Absolute through the Son of God or incarnation (personification of the Absolute or symbolization of Him) can realize and experience God the Father and ultimately the Absolute.

In other religious traditions we find the same approach. Let us consider Hinduism. The Hindus extensively personify and symbolize the Absolute, *Brahman*. They give freedom to individuals to accept any personification or symbol of the Absolute, or "universal consciousness," as Schrödinger calls it.[19] They know that the personification of creative knowledge, the illumining and loving aspects, are all part of the same Absolute. They use symbols for the unification and training of the mind. They also use pictures or statues for the same purpose.[20] Many persons misunderstand the use of symbol, statue, or picture, thinking it idolatry or polytheism. Little do they understand that our ordinary human minds cannot think of the Absolute. We need something tangible so that our minds can think of It. We are in the habit of thinking of things with names, forms, and qualities. So it is impossible for us, generally speaking, to avoid this use of symbol, statue, or picture in the earlier days of our spiritual growth.

In the Buddhistic tradition, the early Buddhists were extreme rationalists. That is the reason they were called ethical idealists. They even avoided discussions of God; they declared that if the mind is trained properly and made one-pointed, the Truth will reveal itself. This means that one becomes aware of the universal consciousness by going beyond the individualized self. However, later on in the history of many such intellectual groups, the necessity for using personifications and symbolizations was recognized. So they used symbols extensively and personified Buddha in place of God. There is nothing wrong in this. Just as the Christians personified Jesus, so did the Buddhists personify Buddha. Other religious groups like Judaism, Islam, and so on, have used symbols suitable to their cultural backgrounds.

There are some individuals who are highly intellectual. They cannot use the emotional approach to religion. They conceive intellectually that there must be a changeless entity behind the changeable world. As Eddington concluded, there must be an Absolute in order to understand the relative.[21] There are many

---

[19] Erwin Schrödinger, *What Is Life?* (New York: The Macmillan Co., 1947).
[20] *Sayings of Sri Ramakrishna.*
[21] A. S. Eddington, *The Philosophy of Physical Science* (New York: The Macmillan Co., 1929).

such personalities in the contemporary world who accept rationally the existence of the Absolute. A great many Hindu philosophers and religious leaders also rationally establish the existence of the Absolute. Rational conclusions and philosophical interpretations, however, do not satisfy those in search of empirical validation of the existence of the Absolute. Therefore, many persons of a highly intellectual temperament seek the verification of this truth. Herein lies also the utility of the use of symbols. In order to verify the existence of God, even from the intellectual point of view of the rationalist, one has to train the mind to be one-pointed. The difficulty arises, even for the Absolutists, in the training of the mind. Since the Absolute is beyond name or form, time and space, qualities and attributes, it cannot be the object of thought. Yet we have to think of something to unify and integrate the mind, for without an integrated mind there is no possibility of valid religious experience to verify the existence of the Absolute. So Hindu thinkers declare that even such personalities must use symbols for the time being, to train the mind for comprehending the Absolute.

As the Hindus describe it, a symbol is a substitute for the Absolute, signifying its universal qualities. They say: "By thinking of the Absolute in something which is not the Absolute but which signifies it, you can know the Truth." We admit that the symbol cannot give a clear idea of the Absolute; however, from psychological necessity we have to use this in order to train the mind. When this mind is made thoroughly one-pointed, the Truth reveals itself. Patanjali, the father of systematic and scientific study of Hindu psychology, emphasized this. When the mind is made one-pointed and thoroughly quiet, free from tension and conflict, anyone, even an atheist, can know the Truth or Absolute.

So we find that all the mature religions use symbols extensively for mental training. But there comes a time, as a person grows psychologically and as his mind is integrated, when he can transcend not only the limitations of the personification of God but also the symbol of the Absolute.

Needless to say, the minds of the vast majority of people belonging to different religions are extremely restless. This restless condition has to be overcome by certain emotional training and the practice of concentration and meditation. Without this, one cannot reach the goal of religion, or attain the knowledge of the Kingdom of God or the manifestation of the divinity that is already in man, or the Truth and manifestation of the love of God.

7

FRUITFUL MEDITATION

There is dynamic power in meditation. We are told by all the great spiritual leaders belonging to different religious traditions that meditation is fruitful and that it is essential for spiritual growth. Yet most of us do not really understand what it is; consequently, we do not know its effect. We all want fruitful results. In the contemporary world, everyone thinks in terms of pragmatism: what is useful and what is practical. Even scholars are always thinking in terms of utility and practicality. In conferences and gatherings with physical and social scientists and philosophers, we find that they always try to stress the practical aspect of what they are discussing. Is religion practical or is it a dream?

Everyone wants practicality. When we talk of meditation, people ask, "What is the pragmatic value of meditation?" Before we go further, we should understand clearly what we mean by meditation, otherwise we cannot understand its pragmatic value or its effect. Often the word "meditation" is loosely used in this country. People say they have been in meditation when they were reading poetry, a prayerbook, or just thinking philosophical thoughts. This may be meditation from their point of view, but it is not the meditation we practice or talk about. When St. Teresa of Avila, St. John of the Cross, George Fox, or John Wesley spoke of contemplation, they did not mean philosophical thought or poetic flight, but something more.

By meditation we mean concentration. Patanjali, the father of Hindu psychology, gives us a clear understanding of concentration and meditation from a scientific point of view:

> At that time (the time of concentration) the seer (Purusha)
> rests in his own (unmodified) state.[22]

---

[22] *Yoga Aphorisms of Patanjali* I: 3 and Swami Vivekananda, *Works*, I, 203.

The first stage of spiritual practices is concentration, according to Patanjali. Concentration means withdrawing the mind from the sense objects and focusing the mind on an aspect of God. As Swami Brahmananda says, in the earlier days of the practice of concentration and meditation or spiritual realization, one must think of God with form and concentrate on Him. "You must meditate upon that one of the many forms of Him you like best."[23] We are in the habit of thinking of things that exist in time and space, that have name, form, qualities, attributes. Our minds are constituted at present in such a way that we can think only of these things. We cannot blame the scientist who said: "God is an abstraction." Of course it is an abstraction to his mind. He does not have any idea of God or Absolute. To Einstein, the atom is not an abstraction; the atom is really real. To you and me it is an abstraction. But if we go to the Massachusetts Institute of Technology, we find that many young people who are making experiments can tell us what the atom is all about. Similarly, we will find that there are persons who are trained in the practice of concentration and meditation. To them God is not an abstraction. God is really real. However, before we can understand the reality of God which is beyond time, space, and causation, the mind must be trained to conceive Him. A personification of God is required. That is the very reason different religions use symbols and substitutes, as we explained in the other chapters. Go to an orthodox Christian church and you will find statues, icons, pictures, crosses, and other symbols. They are absolutely necessary for the vast majority of the people in the beginning of their spiritual life, as we discussed in the chapter, "Psychological Aspects of Religious Symbols." Go to a Buddhistic or Hindu temple, or Jewish synagogue: you will find statues, pictures, or other symbols. They may not be identical, because human beings are different and are brought up in different traditions. They have to take different symbols or substitutes for God or Absolute, accord-

---

[23] *Spiritual Teachings of Swami Brahmananda* (2nd ed.; Mylapore, Madras: Sri Ramakrishna Math, 1933), p. 184.

ing to their own backgrounds, cultural traditions, and mental structure.

Mental structure is a very important factor. A man may be born a Hindu or a Roman Catholic, yet his mental structure may be quite different from others in the same religious tradition. Meister Eckhart was born an orthodox Roman Catholic. He was an official in the Roman Catholic Church. Yet he could not follow the type of rituals and symbols that were used, for, as he grew spiritually, he transcended their limitations. But in the beginning, something tangible with name, form, qualities, and attributes is needed. Hindu teachers point out, as Swami Brahmananda tells us, that one has to take a personification of God in order to focus the mind. When a person focuses the mind, he withdraws it from everyday experiences and objects and places it on an aspect of God or a symbol of God. Before he is established in this practice, the mind wanders and he has to struggle to bring it back to the object of concentration. So in the preliminary stages, in what Patanjali calls *pratyahara*, withdrawing the mind from the objective world and directing it to the object of concentration is called concentration. As a person goes through the period of struggle, the mind gets settled. It takes some time and one has to be patient. Gradually the restless mind becomes quiet and remains focused on the spiritual symbol or ideal; this is called meditation. When the mind does not move about and remains steadily fixed on an aspect of God or a symbol of God, then a person is meditating. Meditation is well-established concentration.

This is a brief description of meditation. Gradually, the aspirant will find that he can go even beyond meditation. As Meister Eckhart declared: "I renounce God for God's sake." (I renounce the personal God for the Absolute.) This great man was grossly misunderstood by the religious authorities, and then he was sent to jail and died there. This would not happen in the Indian tradition. Indian scholars and thinkers realize that there is a state of union beyond personification. However, until that state is attained the individual must steadily continue the practice of concentration and meditation on a personal aspect of God or a symbol of God.

People need symbolism to attract the mind and to help keep it focused. Patience is needed in spiritual practices, because past experiences rise to the surface of the mind. Although these old impressions are in the unconscious, the moment a person tries to meditate, they come up to the conscious level. It is a peculiar reaction. Then these past impressions make the mind more restless for the time being. However, after some time the mind becomes quiet. Then we are established in meditation and reap the pragmatic reward of the practice of concentration and meditation.

The main effect is the realization of God. When the mind is completely focused, then alone can one experience God. The restless mind cannot experience God, cannot even think of God. That is the reason Buddha said in his Fourth Truth that we do not have to speculate about God or discuss Him. The mind must be trained and focused. As Jesus said: "If therefore thine eye be single, thy whole body shall be full of light."[24] This is very important. Patanjali tells us that even agnostics, atheists, and materialists can realize God if they can make their mind one-pointed and single: "There is no limit to the power of the human mind. The more concentrated it is, the more power is brought to bear on one point."[25] According to Patanjali, if anyone can make the mind one-pointed or a complete vacuum and free of all thoughts, then the Truth will reveal itself.

Some of the Buddhists prescribed a method of emptying the mind to eliminate all thought. It is true that if one can negate all thought and make the mind a vacuum without permitting it to become negative, one can reach the Truth, as many Buddhists and some Hindus have done. However, as we mentioned in the chapter on spiritual methods, this method is very difficult even for the intellectual aspirants, because the unconscious mind accumulates the impressions of past experiences and preserves

---

[24] Matthew 6: 22.
[25] Swami Vivekananda, *Works*, I, 130-131.

them. Hindu and Buddhistic psychologists and contemporary dynamic psychologists declare that the major part of mental functions and behavioral activities is motivated by unconscious drives and urges and accumulated impressions. The moment one tries to empty the mind and make it devoid of all positive thought, that moment the unconscious drives and urges come to the surface, creating restlessness of mind and filling it with successive thoughts. Therefore, this method is not generally advocated for the majority of the people. Only a microscopic minority can successfully follow it.

The people who believe in the existence of God, personal or impersonal, should try to focus the mind on an aspect of God; then they will know the truth. If anyone wants to know God or experience God empirically, he has to practice meditation. There is no other way. We tell our scientific friends that if they want to verify these facts and if they want to know the Reality, which is not mere theory nor mere "abstraction," they must go through the training process and discipline. Just as we cannot be an Einstein without making experiments, so we cannot know God without going through this training process of the mind.

Now let us consider the other values. People of the contemporary world are anxious to know the practical utility of mental training and practice of concentration and meditation. Many of them are not so much interested in the knowledge of God as they are in the possibility of more tangible returns. There is tremendous value in the practice of meditation. We know what is happening in the contemporary world. Let us forget psychotic conditions and consider only so-called healthy persons. Wherever we go—whether it is to the garage, a gasoline station, bank, or college—we find that people are suffering from psychosomatic diseases. Recently, when we were in New York, we had a slight accident to our automobile, so we went hurriedly to a garage. The garage man was very nice to us and gave very good advice. But we saw that he was making faces. He explained the reason to us, saying, "I have very bad stomach trouble and pain." I realized what it was, so I said, "You know, you have to try to keep your mind a little quiet. When your mind is restless you can have ulcers." Wherever we go, we meet people who have psychosomatic diseases. Why do they have these? Because the mind is restless; consequently the nerves are affected and do not function properly. As a result, functional diseases develop. Then again, many people cannot rest properly. Often they say, "In the morning I am stiff when I wake up." Even people who occupy high social positions cannot sleep well. They must have sleeping pills. When they get up, they are tired, exhausted. Then they must have a few cups of coffee or something else to stimulate them. Again in the afternoon they must have something for relaxation. They need relaxation because they are tense. Their emotional anxiety, frustration, and disappointments are so strong that their nerves are affected. So they have a little alcoholic beverage or another pill.

Now, if we practice meditation our whole neuromuscular system relaxes while we are doing it. Those who are practicing it know very well that while they are focusing the mind (even though the mind may be restless for the time being), the whole body relaxes. As a result, the nerve tension goes away. While they are meditating they are really breaking the continuity of their unconscious drives and urges. Some people may say, "I am meditating only for ten or fifteen or twenty minutes. What effect can it have throughout the day?" Little do they understand that even though they relax and meditate only for these brief moments two or three times a day, the effect remains. Gradually, the effect is so continuous that it remains with them throughout the day. Their lives become changed. Psychosomatic diseases are completely overcome. Those who are practicing know very well that because they are practicing steadily, the mind is becoming more and more quiet. Some of our scientific friends tell me now, after practicing for some time, for a year or so, "Yes, I see that I am different. I am not so nervous. I am not so tense or stiff." Then they find if they can meditate in the evening for a little while, they do not have to take any drugs to sleep. They fall asleep when they touch the pillow.

In a recent talk on "The Hindu Method of Training the Mind" to the American Association for the Advancement of Psychotherapy, I expounded the idea that if a person is not too far advanced in his mental disturbances, the practice of concentration and meditation can completely eliminate the causes of his disturbances. This was not talk about theories but about the practical aspects. People do not need any tranquilizing medicine then, because the mind becomes tranquil and quiet. Every individual has certain unconscious drives and urges, and every individual has the continuity of his past impressions, but by the practice of meditation this continuity can be broken. The result is wonderful. The whole system is serene. People can have sound sleep. The moment they find that they are getting restless and disturbed because of certain social conditions or certain conditions in the family life and so on, they should sit for a few minutes and think of their Chosen Ideal, repeating the name. Then they will gradually have serenity. And if they can continue this practice, they will find that they can overcome psychosomatic diseases altogether. A man of meditation has no reason to have psychosomatic diseases.

A young man was sent to us by a psychiatrist because of his mental tension. In his childhood he had a very unpleasant experience: a neighbor committed suicide. This created great anxiety in him. During the wartime he married. Unfortunately the marriage failed. The young man was very tense and extremely nervous, apprehensive, and full of anxiety. His whole life was seriously affected. He needed, no doubt, regular counseling. He also needed the practice of concentration. Encouragement gradually affected him. With his practice of concentration he developed courage and enthusiasm. The psychosomatic symptoms gradually began to vanish. In the course of a year or so he became quite normal. Then he also developed courage to meet people. As time went on, and as he got encouragement from us, he married again and settled down in life happily. He often tells us what a tremendous effect he has from this practice of concentration and meditation. We can cite a number of cases of intense anxiety and tension. They gradually overcame these mental problems and also their psychosomatic symptoms.

Then, there is another practical effect. A man or woman of meditation is emotionally stable. Consequently, social relationships are very harmonious. The stable person does not get excited or upset by the behavior of others. He realizes, "Human beings act in this way, but why should I do likewise?" Swami Brahmananda used to tell us that we must not change our attitude and ways of life when other persons act in a harmful manner to us. He also said, "You may do good to a person all your life; yet, if he does not like just one thing you did, he will remember only that and will forget all the good things you did for him." Then he added, "God is just the opposite. You may do all wrong things your entire life; but if you do one good thing, He will use it to lift you up from all wrong actions and thought." Men of God-realization are also like this, as we know from our humble experiences with such personalities.

My master told a very interesting story as an illustration. A holy man was meditating on the bank of a river. When he opened his eyes he saw a scorpion struggling for life in the water. Out of love and compassion for all living beings he went to save its life and picked it up. As he did so, the scorpion stung him, but he took it to the shore just the same and left it on the ground in spite of his great pain. Then he again sat for meditation. Later he opened his eyes and saw the same scorpion back in the river struggling in the current for its life. A second time the holy man picked him up and was stung. However, this time he again saved its life, even though he was in terrible pain. Once more the holy man sat to meditate. Finally, he opened his eyes and there was the scorpion struggling in the river again. This time a thought came to the holy man's mind: "I saved the life of this scorpion twice and twice he has stung me. What should I do now?" Then he reasoned, "It is the nature of the scorpion to sting. It is my nature also to save the life of any living being. He cannot change his nature; why should I change mine?" So for the third time he rescued the scorpion from the current and was stung painfully. Only this time he carried the scorpion far from the bank of the river so it would not jeopardize its life again.

A man of meditation is not upset by destructive people or the disturbing social and political conditions of life. He may seem to be a little disturbed sometimes, temporarily. Swami Shivananda told us one day that a holy man's anger is like a line drawn in water. By the time you finish the line, it is gone. A spiritual man's annoyance or irritation is like that. Because his mind is so quiet, he has thereby the knowledge of the Reality; he does not get upset over the changeable conditions of life.

Another pragmatic effect is this: a man of meditation can influence others because of his serenity. The disturbed person can go to him, sit with him, and in a few minutes he, too, becomes quiet. We have seen time and again people going to Swami Brahmananda, or other great Swamis, with so much heartache: death in the family, disease, or many such other unfortunate conditions. Sitting in the presence of these great spiritual personalities, they become different persons. Their restlessness, misery of mind, and sorrow all vanished. We have seen time and again that such persons leave the presence of the great Swamis with cheerful faces because of their uplifting influence. We know what tremendous influence a man of meditation can have in society. One young woman lost her child through death. She was very much affected by this misfortune and could not eat for several days. Her husband and relatives took her to Swami Shivananda. She was weeping bitterly. Swami Shivananda expressed deep sympathy and love for her. She remained in his presence for some time. Then he gave her offered food and she went home. This visit and being in the great Swami's presence changed her completely. Her heartache and sorrow vanished. Two or three days later she returned to Swami Shivananda and she was an altogether different person. It was indeed an amazing incident. One cannot help but feel the effect of a man of meditation and the consequent love which he spreads because of his meditation.

Another practical value of meditation is that if a man can become established in it through proper practice, his friends and relatives are influenced. In India, when we were small boys, we learned the practice of meditation from the older members of our family, namely, the parents or grandparents who used to practice it. We became interested in the practice of meditation through them. When we were small children, six or seven years old, we used to see them meditating, looking quiet and serene, absorbed in their ideal, and we used to imitate them. This was the beginning of our spiritual life. It can become a great blessing from a pragmatic point of view. It can change even the physical constitution. It can change the mental structure of an individual. It can strengthen the nervous system. It can eliminate all psychosomatic disease, nerve tension, neurotic conditions, psychotic conditions. Finally, it can give the knowledge of God.

As a by-product, it can change society. Society can become peaceful, harmonious. In the contemporary world we find so many disturbances in people. These disturbances cannot be eliminated by sermons, lectures, mass-production conversion, threat of hell, or allurement of heaven. It has to come by changing one's life through the practice of meditation and concentration. By having experience of God, we can change others and make them peaceful, harmonious, and blessed.

8

WHAT IS MYSTICISM?

The word "mysticism" is very much misunderstood in the West, especially in the United States. Some of the outstanding scientific thinkers are very critical of mysticism. Because of the prevalent misunderstanding and misinterpretation, we cannot blame them. In various places one can see how the word is misused, as, for instance, on signs advertising "mystic readings," meaning fortune telling. A few years ago in Atlantic City there was a sign in the window of a place on the boardwalk, "Swami Raja–Reader." This man was a fortune teller.

What do we mean by mysticism? A great American writer and one of the noblest personalities in this country, Dr. Rufus Jones, defines mysticism as:

> ... the type of religion which puts the emphasis on immediate awareness of relation with God, on direct and intimate consciousness of the Divine Presence. It is religion in its most acute, intense, and living stage.[26]

Evelyn Underhill, the great English writer, gives a similar interpretation. According to Dean Inge:

> ... Religious Mysticism may be defined as the attempt to realise the presence of the living God in the soul and nature, or, more generally, as the attempt to realise, in thought and feeling, the immanence of the temporal in the eternal, and of the eternal in the temporal.[27]

Professor Gershom Scholem in *Major Trends in Jewish Mysticism*[28] gives a clear idea of the nature of valid mysticism. Pro-

---

[26] Rufus M. Jones, *Studies in Mystical Religion* (London: Macmillan & Co., 1925), p. xiv.

[27] William Ralph Inge, *Christian Mysticism* (New York: Meridian Books, 1956), p. 5.

[28] Gershom Scholem, *Major Trends in Jewish Mysticism* (New York: Schocken Books, 1946).

fessor David Bakan, in *Sigmund Freud and the Jewish Mystical Tradition*, says:

> This ecstasy, together with its associated content in terms of cognition of the divine, is the aim of Abulafia's meditation. Abulafia is careful to distinguish between this state and wilder states of emotional excitement. As a matter of fact he believes that these other states, which can be confused with the kind of ecstasy that he is talking about, can actually be quite dangerous. In Abulafia's ecstasy it is the 'light of the intellect' which comes in; and for this careful preparation is required.[29]

We fully agree with these Western scholars that real mysticism is direct and immediate experience of God, or Absolute, or Ultimate Reality.

That experience cannot be attained by mechanical means. Certain mechanical methods can produce hallucinations, even religious hallucinations, but not true spiritual experience. As we shall explain later on, real mystical experience reveals the knowledge of the Ultimate Reality and transforms the personality. The use of mechanical means does not integrate the personality; on the contrary, it gradually disintegrates the personality.

How does a person know the difference between a real religious experience and hallucination? scientists and materialistic philosophers want to know. Not long ago in Washington at the Inter-American Congress of Philosophy, one of the philosophers challenged me: "It seems you say that I am God. Then why do I not know that I am God?" Our answer to him was: "It is the veil of ignorance, what the Hindus call cosmic nescience, that makes us forget what we are."

Some psychiatrists and psychologists conclude that all mystical experiences are hallucinations. Once at Bowdoin College in Maine a student came to me after my lecture there and said that his psychiatrist told him that all mystical experiences are hallucinations. The answer for the boy was in the form of a ques-

---

[29] David Bakan, *Sigmund Freud and the Jewish Mystical Tradition* (Princeton, New Jersey: Van Nostrand, 1958), pp. 79-80.

tion: "Is he not having hallucinations himself when he makes such a statement without authentic observation and experimentation?" He may be acquainted with a certain type of psychiatry, but this does not mean necessarily that he is aware of the total mind. It seems that some of these so-called scientists take a narrow viewpoint of anything not within their realm of study. These people should go through the required training and discipline to be capable of evaluating mystical experiences.

The difference between hallucinations and mystical experiences is this: The personality does not change for the better when an individual experiences hallucinations through use of drugs or in mental illness. Mentally ill persons are abnormal and are incapable of behaving in a normal manner. Consider the woman at a Boston mental hospital who thinks she is Mrs. Christ. If she is addressed by her own name, she pays no attention. The moment you say "Mrs. Christ," she approaches you and smiles. A young man that we know lost his balance and thought he was St. Paul returned to the world to spread the message. In a conference of chaplains, a minister reported an experience of his in a mental hospital. A patient approached him and asked, "Who are you?" The chaplain replied, "I am a Christian minister." The man at once said, "Lie down. I am Jesus."

Then there was the elderly woman we knew many years ago who used to come and see us. One day she said, pointing, "I see Jesus there, and I see St. Paul standing there." At the same time her middle-aged daughter had many heartaches caused by her. Now a person who really sees Jesus can never create such trouble for her daughter as we knew happened in this situation. On the contrary, the personality becomes loving, forgiving, peaceful. Such a person cannot have hatred for anyone.

There are two persons in the Christian tradition whom we deeply admire for their endurance, patience, forgiveness, and love, in spite of their being misunderstood and persecuted: St. Francis of Assisi and St. John of the Cross. Few were so greatly persecuted as was St. John of the Cross. He was kept in solitary imprisonment by his own brothers of the Order. However, he did not hurt anyone nor express hatred toward anyone. He remained in his cell, used his beads, and meditated. He was absorbed in God. Eventually, the very persons who persecuted him were changed. Similarly, St. Francis transformed even destructive animals.

We had the privilege of knowing most of the disciples of Sri Ramakrishna and witnessed how they changed personalities. There was the case of the man who went to the Monastery to take away his brother, who became a monk in 1908. The man was angry and drunk and began to abuse the great Swamis. One of the disciples of Sri Ramakrishna, Swami Premananda, went forward and said to him, "Ah, you are so hot!" He sent one of the young Swamis for refreshments and offered them to this man: "Here, take a little cold drink." After a little while he became quiet. Then Swami Premananda told him, "You may take your brother if he wishes to go. We have no objection." Instead, the man stayed for hours. When he was leaving, Swami Premananda gave him a little money and said, "Come again." The very next day he returned. Again, when he was leaving, the great Swami told him, "Come again." Within a few days the man asked permission to remain in the Monastery. Swami Premananda granted him his request and assured him that the Monastery was his home. He finally became a monk and did wonderful work. In about 1915 he founded a hospital in Rangoon which became the most outstanding hospital in that vicinity until the Japanese occupation. After World War II, the Burmese government asked the Ramakrishna Order to build up the hospital again. It is now considered one of the best hospitals in Burma. This Swami is still living and is probably in his eighties by now.

Valid religious experiences may be had by anyone who will go through the necessary practices. Scientists have already trained their minds in concentration. They merely have to change the object of their concentration, that is all. Let us take Sir J. C. Bose as an example. He was one of the greatest contemporary scientists in India who was known all over the world for his scientific contributions. He was the man who discovered that even plants have certain kinds of sensations and reactions. One of his students told us that at certain times he used to be absorbed within himself and completely oblivious of the world. He would forget to eat, and his wife had to go to the laboratory and feed him when he was engrossed in his experiments. He also had what we would call preliminary mystical experiences, perceiving a luminous substance and forgetting the objective world.

So the mind can be made one-pointed through scientific investigation or religious practices advocated by Christians, Hasidic Jews, Buddhists, Hindus, Sufi Muslims, and so on. Buddha Himself declared, "Do not talk about God. Follow the Eightfold Path [which includes the practice of concentration and meditation]. Then you will know the Truth." One of His followers asked Him, "Sir, am I to think that there is no God?" Buddha replied, "Did I say so?" So the disciple asked, "Then am I to expect that there is no God?" Again Buddha replied, "Did I say so?" Philosophically speaking, we cannot say God exists nor can we say God does not exist. Our conception of existence depends on the conception of time, space, and causation. We cannot apply these categories of knowledge to the Absolute. As such, the Absolute is beyond time, space, and causation. So we cannot say that it exists or that it does not exist, because the existence that we perceive is based on the Absolute Existence. Buddha declared that through the Eighfold Path the existence of God or Absolute can be verified. We do not have to speculate on it. We find that the great spiritual leaders belonging to the world's religions verified the existence of God by following individual methods.

Swami Vivekananda was brought up in the Western system of education in Calcutta. He was thoroughly acquainted with the philosophy of John Stuart Mill, Herbert Spencer, and such others. He was acquainted with the philosophical and scientific thinking of his time; consequently, he can be regarded as representative of contemporary thinkers. In his quest for the truth, he went to various religious men and asked the challenging question, "Sir, have you seen God?" No one could give him a satisfactory answer. Then he met Sri Ramakrishna and put the question to Him. He answered, "Yes, I see Him more vividly than I see you, and you can see Him too." We can safely say that this was the beginning of Swami Vivekananda's experimentation in the field of mysticism.

There are various methods of verification of the existence of God. As previously mentioned, the best method is to make the mind one-pointed, single. It is very difficult to achieve. Those who are trying to meditate know very well how difficult it is. Even great philosophers and scientists do not find it easy to keep the mind focused on one thing alone. However, it is certain that without real concentration of mind there can be no valid mystical or religious experience.

Recently, we received a report from a reliable source that a professor of theology, known as a religious leader, discourages people from the practice of concentration. Since he has never practiced it himself, he does not know what it means. Without it he cannot enter the threshold of mystical experience, even though he may discuss religious teachings for hours. When we study the lives of the great leaders of Christianity, from Jesus and the Apostles to St. Paul, St. Bernard, St. Benedict, St. Augustine, St. Francis of Assisi, St. Clara, St. Teresa of Avila, St. John of the Cross, and so on down to George Fox, John Wesley, and such others, we find that every one of them emphasized the practice of concentration on God. They may have used other words, such as contemplation, meditation, or persistent prayer, but all of them had the same meaning in mind—to make the mind one-pointed. We find in *Theologia Germanica:*

> Yet there be certain means thereunto, [to be possessed by the Spirit of God] as the saying is, "To learn an art which thou knowest not, four things are needful." . . . The fourth is to put thy own hand to the work, and practice it with all industry.[30]

St. Teresa writes:

> I may speak of that which I know by experience; and so, I say, let him never cease from prayer who has once begun it, be

---

[30] *Theologia Germanica,* trans. Susanna Winkworth (London: Macmillan & Co., 1874), pp. 74-75.

his life ever so wicked; for prayer is the way to amend it, and without prayer such amendment will be much more difficult. . . . And as to him who has not begun to pray, I implore him by the love of our Lord not to deprive himself of so great a good.[31]

Sufi Islamic leaders, Hasidic and Cabalistic Jews, Hindus and Buddhists also have emphasized this practice.

For thousands of years the Hindus have devoted their time to the discovery of mystical experiences, known also as religious or superconscious experiences. They discovered and perfected the techniques of the different methods suitable to different mental structures. We have to give credit to the Hindus for our present knowledge of these scientific methods. They help us to develop spiritually step by step by using the method most suitable to us. No one should ever be compelled to follow a path not meant for his mental makeup. The results are disastrous. Repulsion and distaste for religion are created in the person.

As we mentioned in a previous chapter, the mind may be classified into four general groups: emotional, intellectual, active, and meditative. These groups are again subdivided, which makes allowance for plenty of freedom. In a Hindu family, we find that some members may worship or meditate on God as the Father of the universe; others take God as Mother, Child, Friend, and so on. Yet all can live in the same household and carry on their functions harmoniously. We saw this in our childhood days.

There are various stages of religious experiences. As we previously mentioned, Sir J. C. Bose had a glimpse of that Reality in the form of a luminous substance. Another great scientist, known to us in the West, has had a similar experience, where it seemed as if the whole world was flooded with light. It seems as if something is there and a thrilling joy fills the mind. This is the first step.

With the second step, a person generally sees a personal as-

---

[31] *The Life of St. Teresa of Jesus*, trans. David Lewis (London: Thomas Baker, 1924), p. 59.

pect of God. This depends on the psychological structure of the individual. (A few do not have this type of experience if they are rationalistic). St. Paul experienced Jesus on his way to Damascus. Some may say that he suffered hallucinations. However, his personality was transformed, and he could no longer remain Saul, the hater of Jesus. He became the founder of Christianity. In a similar way St. Augustine became the founder of Christian theology after his spiritual realization. St. Francis was completely changed after his spiritual experience and could no longer live a carefree life. St. Anthony of Padua used to experience Jesus as a little boy, the Bambino, who walked everywhere with him.

In the third stage, an individual experiences the personal aspect of God with form, qualities, and attributes, while the outside world vanishes from consciousness. Only God and the devotee remain, only He and I. Nothing else exists. Even the body-consciousness is gone. This is called the superconscious state. Both Professor James and Professor Pratt mention this in their books.[32] St. Teresa of Avila describes it from her own experience:

> But our Lord made such haste to bestow this grace upon me, and to declare the reality of it, that all doubts of the vision being a fancy on my part were quickly taken away. . . . For if I were to spend many years in devising how to picture to myself anything so beautiful, I should never be able, nor even know how to do it; for it is beyond the reach of any possible imagination here below; the whiteness and brilliancy alone are inconceivable. . . . It is a light so different from any light here below that the very brightness of the sun we see, in comparison with the brightness and light before our eyes, seems to be something so obscure, that no one would ever wish to open his eyes again.[33]

In the fourth stage of religious experience, or the second stage

---

[32] William James, *The Varieties of Religious Experience* (New York: Longmans, Green & Co., 1929). See also James B. Pratt, *The Religious Consciousness* (New York: The Macmillan Co., 1945) and *Psychology of Religion* (New York: The Macmillan Co., 1907).

[33] *The Life of St. Teresa of Jesus*, p. 248.

of superconscious realization, duality vanishes. There is only one Existence. "I" no longer exists; only that Existence remains. Many rationalistic thinkers, particularly the scientists, would no doubt like to have this experience. They are not interested in a personal aspect of God. They cannot conceive that there is a personal Being; but at the same time they accept the existence of the Absolute or Universal Consciousness. This is natural to their mental constitution. It is possible for them to train their minds and to attain that state. Then they know that there is something behind the phenomenal world, something permanent behind the changeable entities. The world is not, after all, a mere succession of sensations, events, or changeable conditions.

There is yet another state, discussed by Swami Brahmananda, in which one enters a state beyond duality, beyond unity. It is called the *blissful* superconscious state, beyond all description. We can only know what it is by experiencing it. Take, for instance, love. It is indescribable. To know it, a man must experience it. So it is with the fifth state of mystical experience. A person becomes intoxicated with it. It is so consuming that he feels complete, full. He becomes all-loving toward every being. His whole personality is thoroughly changed.[34]

Some people are afraid of mysticism, thinking that it will make them "other-worldly." There are also some who are afraid to meet a mystic or even to marry a man or woman who is interested in mysticism, because "he will not love me then." To use strong language, they are stupid to think this way; they do not know what they are talking about. The individual who has real mystical experience or who is striving for that becomes a center of love. He does not withdraw himself from the world; he becomes one with it. He has such tremendous power because of that love of God that he becomes a universal lover, a real lover. He can give his life for his wife; the wife can give her life for the husband; and so on. He has no ego; he feels the pres-

---

[34] Swami Brahmananda, *Spiritual Teachings*. See also Swami Vivekananda, *Works*.

ence of God in all and so he can love all. Even with the first stage of spiritual experience, with just a glimpse of that Reality, a person cannot help but love. So it can be imagined to what extent love will grow with the higher stages of mystical experiences.

There are some critics belonging to certain religious groups who think that real experience of God can be attained only through their particular sect or methods. Some of them often make a distinction between what they call "Christian" mysticism and "Oriental" mysticism. They also try to show that there are differences in the mystical experiences of different religious traditions. However, when we study the lives of the great mystics belonging to different religions, we find that their experiences are similar, as we have explained in the *Hindu View of Christ*.[35] They differ only in circumstances, but not at all in their real nature, quality, or effect on the individual. The differences are in the mental constitutions of the individuals rather than in the religions. For instance, personalistic or devotional mystics of any religion will experience the personal aspect of God, whether it is Jesus, Buddha, Krishna, Ramakrishna, or some other such personality. The effect of such experiences on the personality is the same. The individual is thoroughly integrated; his emotions are stabilized; his inordinate tendencies are wiped out. He expresses the highest ethical principles, and above all, universal love. The rationalistic mystics belonging to different religions have similar experiences of union with the Absolute. They lose their individuality and become absorbed in the Absolute, just as a spoonful of water is poured into the infinite ocean. When we dispassionately observe and study the different types of mystics, we are compelled to accept that the differences exist as a result of their mental constitution rather than religious affiliation or historical background.

Two different persons can also have the same realization at the same time. This happened to Swami Brahmananda and

---

[35] Swami Akhilananda, *Hindu View of Christ* (New York: Philosophical Library, 1949).

Swami Vivekananda. We heard the details from Swami Brahmananda himself, although he used to be reticent about telling his personal experiences. One day he was sitting outside the Belur Math (monastery) facing the Ganges. He had an exalted experience of the Divine Mother. At that time, Swami Vivekananda was returning to the Math from Calcutta on a small boat. He also had the same experience simultaneously with Swami Brahmananda even though they were in separate places. He arrived at the Math full of joy, thrilled by his experience. He decided to perform a public ceremony in the monastery. He never did anything without consulting Swami Brahmananda, so he went to him and addressed him, saying, "We should have this worship." Swami Brahmananda was so intoxicated by his experience that he could not give a proper answer. He replied, "All right, we shall talk about it tomorrow morning."

Another criticism voiced in regard to mystics like the Hindu monists or some schools in Buddhism is that they are negative. There is considerable misunderstanding in the West, not only regarding these particular schools of mysticism but also of mysticism in general in the Oriental countries. A monistic Hindu no doubt considers the world to be relative and seeks the Ultimate Reality. But when he realizes that Reality, he finds Its presence in all. Consequently, he becomes a lover of all individuals who are on the relative plane. In contemporary history, Swami Vivekananda demonstrated that he was a universal lover of mankind, even though he was originally a monist.

Some mystics start with devotional methods; and, after realizing God in a personal aspect, they go on to complete union with their ideal in the fourth and fifth stages of superconscious experience. Others start with the monistic or nondualistic attitude in their practices; and, after attaining the state of union, they return to the devotional stage of mystical experiences. Swami Brahmananda and Swami Vivekananda and other such personalities are great examples of this intermingling of mystical experiences and manifestation of intense love for mankind, which has been mentioned in another chapter. The life of Sri Ramakrishna is a scientific demonstration that the various religious practices prescribed in the different religions can lead to valid religious experiences. Those experiences are not hallucinations nor hypnotic spells but are validated by empirical facts. This proves that there is no real conflict between scientific method and valid mystical methods.

There is another question in the minds of many noble personalities who are deeply interested in the welfare of society, the question of whether mysticism and spiritual practices as are discussed in previous chapters are not valuable merely to individuals. They often challenge us that these devotional practices cannot help us to solve the contemporary social, national, international, and interracial problems. In fact, directly or indirectly they emphasize humanism. Many of these persons are very noble souls and are trying to help society. Yet we must say they do not fully realize the effect of devotional practices and mystical realizations in society. When we study the history of Christianity, we find that men like St. Francis of Assisi, George Fox and others are the people who started real welfare work or humanitarian work. Their source of inspiration was the experience of God. As Sri Ramakrishna repeatedly said, when you find God within yourself, you find Him in the universe. His spiritual experience cannot be measured by our limited minds, but it was He who really inspired Swami Vivekananda and other great disciples in the service of man. Swami Vivekananda and his brother swamis were the first people who started welfare work of various types toward the end of the last century in India. Their experience of God made them feel the presence of God in all, so they could love and serve every man belonging to any religion or any race. Then, we find that Mahatma Gandhi, who was also inspired by the lives of Sri Ramakrishna and Swami Vivekananda, lived an intense spiritual life of devotional practices. He could do wonderful welfare work because of his love for man. The history of Buddhism shows us that the people who lived the life of intense spiritual practices were the first people to start organized philanthropic work in the history of mankind. Similar instances can be found in other religious traditions. So we emphatically say that spiritual practices and mystical realizations do not make one selfish or self-centered; they expand one and make one love and serve mankind.

If our noble friends who are deeply interested in welfare work want to have really effective humanitarian activity, they must also intensify certain forms of spiritual practices according to their own temperaments. (We admit that they do not have to follow some of the conventional religious methods.) We say again that mystical experiences and devotional practices do not make one isolated or self-centered; on the contrary, they make one universal.

9

RELIGION IN EVERYDAY LIFE

There is widespread misconception about religion and its value. Consequently, many persons cannot clearly understand its place in everyday life. Some seem to think that religion means the acceptance of certain creeds and dogmas, or belief in certain personalities, or repeating, "Lord, Lord."[36]

We know that many Western thinkers have revolted against religion, saying that it is an opiate and that designing individuals take advantage of those who are under its influence. In the pages of European history we find that innocent, illiterate persons were exploited by those who were not only supposed to be religious but who were also associated with religious organizations. We cannot blame the critics for their reactions when the masses revolted against organized religion. They found that the exploiters received the support of organized religion for their activities. They were told that even though they were suffering in this life they would enjoy peace and happiness in heaven. This kept them subdued and in a way powerless to assert themselves.

There have also been many abuses in the name of religion in other parts of the world. Exclusive rights and privileges have been claimed by some who preyed on the ignorant, so that a large class of people remained in a miserable state—physically, mentally, and spiritually.

In Europe, the revolt against religion was levelled against the Judeo-Christian tradition. In both Europe and America we find that very few have studied Oriental religions, especially Hinduism and Buddhism. When Westerners criticize religion, they generalize without consideration of the contribution of other

---

[36] Matt. 7: 11.

religions. Again, the people in the Orient, nurtured in European tradition for the last century and influenced by European scholars, accepted unconditionally the criticism against religion levelled by European scholars. This uncritical attitude on the part of Oriental countries like India and China created a great deal of confusion in the minds of thoughtful young people in those countries. They began to consider that religion was the cause of their degradation under imperialism and their misery on the material plane. They were also influenced by those in the West who were patronizing the people of the East and encouraging them—with definite political and industrial motivation—to stick to their religion, while letting the West take care of their physical welfare.

Once the criticism against Christianity is evaluated properly, then we can determine whether or not other religions can contribute anything to our everyday life. We should consider whether the abuses that are criticized by the humanistic Marxists are the inherent qualities of Christianity or the accrued abuses. If they are inherent qualities, then we can safely say that Christianity is incompatible with modern technological and industrial civilization. If they are not inherent, the critics have no justification for condemning Christianity.

In the Sermon on the Mount we do not find any justification for the exploitation of others. Jesus tells us to love God and our neighbor. In loving our neighbors we do something for them as our real Self. Jesus never specified that we must love only Gentiles or Jews, Europeans or Asiatics, white or dark. He was universal. He meant His teachings for all, without distinctions as to caste, creed, class, or race. So when He said, "Love thy neighbor," He meant all neighbors, not just this or that type of person—not just my family, to the exclusion of your family. He meant that we should love all persons as the veritable manifestations of the real Self.

In His practical life, Jesus demonstrated that love is applicable in everyday life. One interesting factor we observe in the lives of great personalities or incarnations is that they do not utter a word that is not demonstrated by them in their lives.

Their teachings become powerful because they are supported by their activities. Take the various passages of the Sermon on the Mount. We find that every one of them was fulfilled in the life of Jesus. When anyone wanted to exercise a method other than the religious, He opposed and stopped them, just as he did not allow St. Peter to use violence in spite of real provocation. We know that He showered His blessings on Judas and did not exclude him from the Last Supper, even though He was aware that Judas would betray Him and become an instrument of His crucifixion.

If we review the various incidents of His life, we shall find that every one of the utterances of Jesus was justified and exemplified in His life. "Blessed are the pure in heart, for they shall see God." Do we find any trace of impurity in Him, or any envy, hatred, jealousy, selfishness, lust, greed? They were all banished from the mind and existence of Jesus. He also trained his disciples accordingly, so that they could be thoroughly established in purity. When impure persons approached Him, He gave them His love and blessings. He did not make any distinction between saint and sinner. It is said in the *Bhagavad-Gita* that a wise man does not make such a distinction: "He attains excellence who looks with equal regard upon well-wishers, friends, foes, neutrals, arbiters, the hateful, the relatives, and upon the righteous and unrighteous alike."[37]

Jesus always used the spiritual approach to the problems of life. When two or more persons live together, there will be conflict and disturbance among the personalities. No two persons are alike mentally. They do not have the same likes and dislikes, the same attitudes, the same sense of responsibility. Consequently, there will be problems arising from contacts with other human beings. When such disturbances arise, a man can take either the spiritual or non-spiritual method in handling them. A religious person must always use the spiritual method under all conditions and circumstances. External conditions should not change his way of life; otherwise, he is not a religious man.

---

[37] *Srimad-Bhagavad-Gita* VI: 9.

We do not find anything in the life and teachings of Jesus to justify the abuses of Christianity that have occurred in the past centuries. Yet, unfortunately, as time rolled on, many people could not live up to the highest religious ideals. They began to justify their iniquities by stretching and distorting the text of the teachings of Jesus, promising themselves heaven in the life hereafter.

The common man has been exploited in various ways, both socially and economically. Violent fighting has been used in the solution of interracial and international problems. This anti-religious spirit, expressed at different periods in different countries in the name of religion, is not what Jesus or his great followers—from St. Paul, St. Francis, and others to George Fox and John Wesley—advocated. The Dark Ages in Europe give us a very sad picture of Christianity until St. Francis, St. Anthony, and such others appeared. Neither Christianity nor Jesus can be held responsible for such abuses. Unfortunately, abuses of religion occur in every society. When a great religious leader is born, human minds are lifted to a higher plane. Many follow his teachings and carry out the ideals he teaches in everyday life. Again, in the course of time, mankind forgets the ideals and begins to act deplorably, as happened in the Spanish Inquisition.

The abuses that have been carried out in different parts of Europe, the exploitation of the weak by the strong, cannot be justified, as some religious leaders and thinkers try to do. We all know how some of the Western leaders have tried to lead the Oriental and African countries to believe that they were the burden of the white race, while at the same time they were exploiting these people.

We agree that the teachings of Jesus do not support such abuses; but the critic asks, "Why should we cling to religion when there is so much bloodshed and destruction in the name of religion?" They claim to believe in the utility of a moral life, but they would like to establish a life of brotherhood without the affiliation with any established conception of religion. They become materialistic or atheistic humanists, advocating morality and welfare work, with no real conception of God.

Bertrand Russell and Julian Huxley advocate religion without revelation, or mere ethical culture. They want a religion of ethics and humanism. They do not go beyond that. They mean well, as we can see in their writings,[38] but historical evidence proves that their viewpoint cannot really stabilize society. Humanistic ideas fail within a short time. Buddhistic humanism could stand, because it emphasized the search for truth as the primary objective of life. Buddha advocated the Eightfold Path: right comprehension, right resolution, right speech, right action, right way of living, right efforts, right thoughts, and right meditation. He also advocated actual transformation of the way of life.

The viewpoints of Julian Huxley,[39] Bertrand Russell, and previous thinkers like Compte and Babcock have not resulted in stabilizing the personality; consequently the everyday life of the people remains unaffected. They are still selfish, self-centered, egotistic, even though they discuss humanism. We cannot find a better example of this than the late Mr. Stalin and others like him, who advocated humanism but failed to express it because they did not change their way of life and their values of life. Humanism based on a sensate attitude or materialistic point of view is bound to degenerate. We say that it is not the fault of any individual, but it is a defect in the attitude of life and its application. People may claim to be associated with religious institutions, but if they do not apply religious principles, as advocated by great religious leaders, they will continue to behave as they are doing.

The main objective of religion is verification of the existence of the Ultimate Reality or God. Real religion and mystical experience are identical. Ethical living and humanism are only

---

[38] Bertrand Russell, *Why I Am Not A Christian* (New York: Simon and Schuster, 1957).

[39] Julian Huxley, *Religion Without Revelation* (New York: Harper & Bros., 1957).

means to that end; they are not what we understand as the real goal of religion.

These great scholars mean well so far as their personal attitude toward religion goes. However, those who entertain such ideas have overlooked the fact that it is the religious people in the world who have established the true spirit of brotherhood, stabilized society, strengthened family relationships and ties, and built up human character and integrated human personality. What we call brotherhood, the equality to which we aspire, and similar ideals, are direct contributions of religious personalities. We know that the ideals advocated by the humanists are based on the teachings of Krishna, Buddha, Jesus, and Ramakrishna. When we analyze the noble sentiments in human society we can trace them all to these personalities. They are the ones who lived the ideals as they taught them.

We must try to understand and practice these religious ideals in our everyday life. The ideals in themselves are obviously constructive, not destructive; but those who do not live according to the ideals become destructive and abusive. So our advice to Occidental and Oriental critics of religion is that they should not condemn anything without knowing it properly, without having first-hand knowledge of it through practice. Very little of religion can be understood without practicing it, just as the value of scientific discoveries cannot be understood without experimentation in the laboratory. So it is that religion cannot be properly evaluated until those principles are applied in everyday life.

It has also been said that religion cannot be applied to life in this industrial civilization, that it is practicable only for the perfectionist or the medieval monastery. Reinhold Niebuhr wrote:

> Ambiguous methods are required for the ambiguities of history. Let those who are revolted by such ambiguities have the decency and consistency to retire to the monastery, where medieval perfectionists found asylum.[40]

Another well-known religious leader abandoned the princi-

---

[40] Reinhold Niebuhr, *Christianity and Power Politics*, p. 175.

ples of religion at the time of World War II. Karl Barth wrote at the time:

> The Churches ought today to pray in all penitence and sobriety to bear witness to all the world that it is necessary and worthwhile to fight and to suffer for this *just peace*.
>
> . . . .
>
> It is precisely Christian thought which insists that resistance should be offered, and it is the Christians themselves who must not withhold their support. . . . The cause which is at stake in this war is our cause. . . . The Christians who do not realize that they must take part unreservedly in this war must have slept over their Bibles as over their newspapers.[41]

Our answer to such ideas is that religion is not obsolete; its principles are valid at any time. Unfortunately, men and women drift away from the teachings of great spiritual personalities in various religions, even though they remain associated with the church, temple, synagogue, or mosque, and though many of them are the custodians of religion. When the basic ideals of religions are forgotten, the people become full of conflict, tension, and frustration. Consequently, they develop psychoneuroses and psychosomatic diseases. Interpersonal, interracial, interreligious, and international problems are created. Moreover, life becomes extremely miserable.

The objective of religion is the awareness of God in our everyday life. We beg to differ from those who seem to think that this awareness will come only in life after death. Neo-Orthodox thinkers take the attitude of a few centuries ago and console human beings with the thought that even though they cannot follow religious principles now, they can take the name of God and surrender themselves to the "historical Jesus" in the utter agony of their helplessness and sin. Then they can have peace in the next world. Jesus definitely refutes such ideas of Neo-Orthodoxy. "Not everyone that saith, 'Lord, Lord' shall enter into the Kingdom of Heaven, but he that doeth the will of the Father in Heaven."[42]

---

[41] Barth, *This Christian Cause*, chap. 1.
[42] Matt. 7: 21.

This very statement implies that our life in [...]
with religious ideas and ideals. The substance of reli[...]
is consciousness of the presence of God, as experience[...]
Brother Lawrence. As Sri Ramakrishna tells us, we must li[...]
in this world in the awareness of God.

> As a boy holding to a post or pillar whirls about it with head-
> long speed without fear of falling, so perform thy worldly
> duties, fixing thy hold firmly upon God, and thou shalt be free
> from danger. . . . So be in the world, but always remember
> Him.[43]

Many centuries before the advent of Buddha, Sri Krishna
described *Karma Yoga*, or the path of action, in the *Bhagavad-
Gita*. He explained that by performing duties in the world in
the spirit of service and dedication without caring for the results, one can attain the knowledge of God.

> Being steadfast in Yoga, . . . perform actions, abandoning at-
> tachment, remaining unconcerned as regards success or failure.
> This evenness of mind (in regard to success and failure) is
> known as Yoga.
> . . . .
> Endued with this evenness of mind, one frees oneself in this
> life, alike from vice and virtue.
> . . . .
> The wise, possessed of this evenness of mind, abandoning the
> fruits of their actions, freed forever from the fetters of birth,
> go to that state which is beyond all evil.
> . . . .
> Therefore, do thou always perform actions which are obliga-
> tory, without attachment;—by performing action without at-
> tachment, one attains to the highest.[44]

Sri Krishna also declared that every individual, by virtue of
his birth, has to perform certain duties: (1) to God, (2) to
spiritual leaders who teach the religious ideal, (3) to parents
and grandparents, (4) to fellow human beings, (5) to other liv-

---

[43] *Sayings of Sri Ramakrishna* XXXIV: 631.
[44] *Srimad-Bhagavad-Gita* II: 46, 50, 51; III: 19.

...th, Buddha emphasizes the right ...s a means for knowing the Truth. ...e Buddhists is much deeper and more ...umanism, advocated by Compte, Bab- ...ry thinkers we have mentioned. Materi- ...not withstand the temptations of human life. ...g person may start helping others and doing good fo... ...mon man; but he loses his understanding of the welfare ...umanity in a very short time and places himself in an authoritarian position, indulging in most unhumanistic or inhuman activities, almost on the level of brutes. Utilitarian and pragmatic humanism does not become really effective unless it is based on either Buddhistic ethical idealism or religious ideal-ism. History reveals that humanism of the materialistic or prag-matic type cannot sustain the stability of an individual in human fellowship and brotherhood. That is the reason why in this modern age Sri Ramakrishna declared that we must install God in our lives and then perform our duties. Sri Krishna gave the same idea about 1000 B. C. If we can accept this viewpoint, then alone can we have a stabilizing power in our lives.

Human beings are interrelated and related to God, just as the rays of the sun have a relationship to each other and to the sun. This very ideal is the basis of happiness in our everyday life. Swami Vivekananda's principle of *Karma Yoga* (path of action for God-realization) shows us that we should cultivate the presence of God in and through our activities, regardless of their nature. It is essential that we have the awareness and knowledge of God; then we may perform our duties, and our lives will be harmonious. The type of work we do is not so important, reli-gious or otherwise; it is our attitude that counts. When we have the knowledge of God, all work, no matter what it may be, is converted into worship. Every man and woman cannot enter a monastery or convent, nor is it necessary that everyone become a monk or a nun. It is more important to become aware of God.

The real spirit of religion is not in negating life and the world, but in perceiving God in and through the world. In the Indian tradition, a butcher reached the highest truth by carrying on his work in the spirit of service and in performing his duties to his father. A king also reached the highest truth by performing his duties in the spirit of dedication. We know a lady who attained the highest superconscious state by performing her duties as a wife and mother, at the same time carrying on her spiritual practices and devotional exercises. There have been many such instances in other religious traditions.

This brings us to the question: How can we remain aware of God in performing our everyday duties when we have so many things to do? In American life we find that although this country offers all the opportunities for meeting one's physical needs, everyone has to struggle for an existence. Their time is spent in working, keeping themselves fit for work, in recreation, in raising families, and so on. *How much time is left for their cultural activities, and above all, for their spiritual exercises?* They find it very difficult to give any time to intellectual pursuits, cultural activities, and religious development. Is there a solution, or is religion meant for only a few? Our answer is that religion—Christian, Hindu, Buddhist, Jewish, Islamic—is meant for all persons, regardless of race, color, or nationality. Everyone can find a way to apply religious principles to his everyday life.

Those who are working in the world must cultivate a new outlook on life and apply the religious ideal in their everyday activities, remaining aware of the presence of God in what they do. It is essential to remember that we are all to serve the all-loving God in various ways. As Jesus told His followers, we must love God and our neighbor. When we bring this principle into our lives it is not difficult to remember God. It requires effort and struggle to become aware that it is He who is receiving our worship in the industrial plant, the office, or the classroom. So we must constantly remind ourselves that we are serving Him, whether in the kitchen, department store, law office, hospital, or school, since all members of society are veritable manifestations of God. Knowing this, we have to translate the idea into action.

There are many who say that when a man takes care of his family he is doing his duty and has no time to devote to religion other than going to weekly services in the church, temple, or synagogue. However, weekly attendance at a religious service does not necessarily make a person religious, although it is helpful. Even if a person thinks of God during the worship, if he does not do so during the rest of the week in his secular activities, then there is a dichotomy which prevents the individual from becoming truly religious. Life cannot be divided into secular and spiritual departments; it is either one or the other. It is the awareness of God that makes the difference, not necessarily attendance at religious ceremonies, though such attendance is important.

There are many persons in different communities of this country who hold important positions in church organizations, yet they are actually irreligious. In a recent discussion with us, a gentleman enumerated prominent people in this country who have accumulated enormous wealth in questionable industrial activities and who have then given large contributions to various organizations, including the church, particularly for missionary work in rescuing the "heathen." It is true that these contributions were generous and no doubt consoling to the givers, but this kind of generosity did not necessarily make them religious or true followers of Jesus. It is in their lives that we look for evidence of awareness of the religious ideal. A man may have very little of this world's goods and yet be aware of God and love mankind. With that, if he gives only a few grains of rice to others, the act becomes deeply spiritual. If he has nothing to give, his love, prayers, and kind thoughts for the welfare of others are a blessing to the world.

There have been many instances in Indian history of humble contributions for the good of mankind which were made by spiritual persons. Pavhari Baba is an example from the second half of the last century. He lived in a cave with hardly any possessions, yet he lived an intense spiritual life and shared what he had with the people, and he changed any man or woman with whom he came in contact.

There is another question to consider regarding the application of religious principles to social, national, and international problems. We know that trouble is arising in Asiatic countries: India, Egypt, Indonesia, and other places. In order to solve such problems, one of two methods can be used. The first is the aggressive, militaristic, imperialistic method; the second is the spiritual. There are persons who claim spiritual motivation in establishing an empire. Either they do not know religious ideals or they deceive themselves. This aggressive method cannot solve national or international problems; if such were the case there would not have been so much dissension and so many wars in the West for the last two thousand years. Dr. Pitirim Sorokin and Dr. Howard Mumford Jones have clearly shown this in their thought-provoking books.[45]

Aggression has been tried time and time again and it has failed repeatedly. It is bound to fail because it is based on selfishness, greed, and love of power. With these qualities, a person cannot possibly care about the welfare of others; only antagonism is created. The last two wars show how this happens. There are thinkers who are apprehensive that there will be a third world war. It is bound to come if the cause of war is not removed. So there is really only one way out. We must introduce the religious ideals into national and international relations.

We have considered the religious ideal in interpersonal relationships or in love of neighbor, but some may wonder if it is possible to apply the religious principle in collective life. It is true that it is easier to carry it out individually, but we can also control greed, love of power, hypocrisy, insincerity, and dishonesty in our collective life.

Human beings are greatly influenced by towering spiritual

[45] Pitirim A. Sorokin, *The Crisis of Our Age* (New York: E. P. Dutton, 1945), p. 205; Pitirim A. Sorokin and Walter A. Lunden, *Power and Morality* (Boston: Porter Sargent, 1959); Howard Mumford Jones, *Education and World Tragedy* (Cambridge, Mass.: Harvard University Press, 1946).

personalities. We know that the blessings of the world have been introduced by them at different periods in history. Sri Krishna tells us that whatever a great man does, the masses follow. "Whatsoever the superior person does, that is followed by others. What he demonstrates by action, that people follow."[46] So, if one lives an intensely spiritual life, his example will be followed by others. Gandhi is an outstanding example of this. During the lifetime of Jesus only a handful of persons actually followed his teachings, but through them the thought of that period was changed. The same is true of the influence of Buddha. His wonderful message of the conquest of hatred by love was carried out in the life of the people for centuries. Such personalities spread the religious ideals among the masses through their immediate followers, and thus create a rise in the whole culture.

By following the spiritual ideal, it was possible for the Quakers to establish a city of brotherly love. We all know what William Penn did for the American Indians. There are also others in the Christian tradition who have spread the spirit of brotherly love. In recent years the Quakers have demonstrated this ideal in their work in many countries, including the so-called "enemy" territories, during the hostilities of World War II. Even in those countries they were considered the salt of the earth. In these Quakers we find the true spirit of Jesus.

Mahatma Gandhi found his inspiration in Krishna, Buddha, Jesus, Ramakrishna, and Swami Vivekananda. He lived an intensely spiritual life with an awareness of the presence of God and he demonstrated the ideal of Buddha that "hatred cannot be conquered by hatred, but by love." He worked on a high spiritual level for the solution of Indian social problems and also for the attainment of Indian freedom from the greatest imperialistic country of the contemporary world. We know that the British rulers persecuted him and his followers in a most brutal way. Still, this great man stuck to the ideal of non-violence, non-cooperation, and manifestation of soul force. The

[46] *Srimad-Bhagavad-Gita* III: 21.

masses of India were inspired by him and they reached the collective goal of independence by non-violent methods. This historical event justifies our statement that the spiritual ideal can ultimately help us to have both individual and collective peace of mind in a spiritual society.

We can refer to another glorious example in history in the life of Ashoka, Emperor of India, in about 300 B.C. After being converted to Buddhism, this great soul was thoroughly changed and followed the principle of conquest of hatred by love. The ideal spread like wildfire and thoroughly transformed the collective mentality of greater India, which remained peaceful for several centuries.

It is almost unbelievable that spiritual power can have such magnetic influence over human beings, but it justifies the statement made by Swami Vivekananda: "Human beings are basically divine." It is the duty of spiritual leaders to bring out the spiritual potentialities of the people to manifest their divine qualities by leading spiritual lives.

Toward the end of the last century, Swami Vivekananda dynamically emphasized that practical Vedanta and *Karma Yoga* (path of action) are the real solutions to individual and collective problems. In fact, he foresaw the contemporary world wars and predicted that the application of Vedantic principles of the oneness of man (in God) would be the only solution for peace in collective life.

It does not matter what some of the so-called religious leaders like Barth, Niebuhr, and Temple may say about religious ideals being meant for the medieval perfectionists. Historical evidences point to the errors in their diagnoses of and remedies for contemporary problems. Contrary to their view, the statements of Jesus: "Blessed are the meek . . . the peacemakers . . . the poor in spirit . . ." are valid, as shown in previous paragraphs. These ideals are meant not only for the "perfectionists," but for all people all over the world in all ages. In fact, if we do not follow these principles individually and collectively we are bound to face emotional disintegration and collective destruction.

Religion must be applied in everyday life. Individual and

family life cannot be integrated or harmonized without the spirit of religion. Almost every family is affected by mental and emotional problems, some more than others. In the course of ten or fifteen years we shall see what happens to the family structure in this country unless living customs and attitudes revert to religious principles.

Again, the problems of labor and management cannot be solved unless religious principles are applied by both labor and management in seeking solutions. Both groups must cultivate spiritual vision and the spirit of cooperation and coordination. The mutual contribution of knowledge, skills, efficiency for the service of humanity is essential.

National and racial problems are very serious now. These can be solved only by applying the spiritual principles in our everyday life—the sooner the better—for ourselves, our families, our community, our nation, and the world. Then alone can humanity find peace.

SRI RAMAKRISHNA
AND MODERN PSYCHOLOGY

SRI RAMAKRISHNA
AND MODERN PSYCHOLOGY

by

SWAMI AKHILANANDA

Offered to
SWAMI BRAHMANANDAJI MAHARAJ
with humble salutations
and loving devotion

This is the occasion of the celebration of the one-hundredth anniversary of the birth of Sri Ramakrishna, a veritable embodiment of religious understanding and realization. He was born in India in 1836 at a very significant time; just when Western scientific movements were approaching India. That was actually the time when English education, instead of Sanskrit and indigenous education, was introduced into India. Western civilization with its scientific methods and outlook was slowly influencing modern-educated men and women. Atheism, skepticism and other forms of thought, the necessary result of materialistic and objective culture and totally alien to Indian civilization and Indian people, were just beginning to affect her people. It is also a very significant fact that at this time Christian movements were aggressively introduced into India. As a result there was need of a great personality to harmonize these Eastern

This lecture, delivered at the Plantations Auditorium on the Centenary Celebration of Sri Ramakrishna, was published by The Vedanta Society, Providence, Rhode Island, 1937.

and Western cultural outlooks and activities: in brief, Science and Religion, and also, apparently conflicting religious ideals and practices.

The objective study and use of the material forces of nature, of steam, electricity, etc., thoroughly revolutionized the West. In spite of the immense good these brought in the form of material prosperity and comfort, they seriously affected the religious and social values of life. As a result, an unconscious demand was felt in the West for re-emphasis on the spiritual values and experiences of life.

The West stands for scientific thought, discoveries, achievements. Although Christianity is taken up by the West, the land of Christianity is not the West, it is in fact Asia. India stands for spiritual idealism and meditation and is the place of spiritual culture. We find that since the advent of Sri Ramakrishna, East and West have mingled very intimately. In spite of all differences, we are brought together. Some think that, due to English rule, and others think that, due to scientific improvement, we are brought together. It is a fact, however, that we are together and cannot really be separated one from the other. The life of Sri Ramakrishna harmonizes not only different religious and racial groups but also different cultural groups.

Sri Ramakrishna was born in a very devout family. In his childhood he imbibed the traditional spiritual culture and atmosphere. He stands actually for the Hindu ideal of life. Again, he also stands for Western scientific and rationalistic mentality. We find in him the development of intuitive realization, which we call superconscious experience, as well as the scientific approach to the problems of life. He lived just like a Hindu boy and devoted himself to spiritual realization. In his boyhood, when he was sent to primary school, he inquired if that education would give him anything more than bread and butter. When he realized that it would only give bread and butter and worldly comforts he at once gave up school, saying, "This has nothing to do with me. I do not care for education that means only bread and butter."

This outlook shows that Sri Ramakrishna was the pragmatist of all modern pragmatists. He evaluated things from the highest point of view in life. To him, if any form of education or any activity would not give the highest culture of the soul, then it was not practical or really useful. Since his boyhood Sri Ramakrishna would always judge the practical value and utility of a course of action before applying it in life. Once convinced of the real value he would apply it thoroughly and never give it up.

When he heard about God from his mother and other persons, he told himself, "If there is God, I must see Him, I must experience Him, otherwise there is no meaning of God in my life and He will remain always limited to books and to Scriptures or to the teachings of religious leaders and parents." He therefore devoted himself to the realization of God. In that respect he was thoroughly scientific. He wanted direct and immediate knowledge of God. We learn later how scientific he was in his spiritual life, devotional methods and also in his inner divine experiences. He is, therefore, not only an inspirer of India, but equally an inspirer of other parts of the world. As time goes on, we shall realize more fully the effect of that life. Christians, Hindus, Jews, Mohammedans, Buddhists and all others are benefited by his emphasis on the fundamental principles of life, religion and action and man's relation to the Supreme Being, and to his fellow beings.

Sri Ramakrishna through his spiritual experiences understood the unity of existence, and found that the different religions were so many paths to the ultimate realization of God. He saw that all these different groups were worshipping the same Truth.

There are many persons who have peculiar ideas about God and also about mystic experiences. Mystic experiences are actually the basis of religion. They give a direct experience and realization of God. This is the only way we can have first-hand religion. Mystic realization will make us better persons, better citizens and true lovers of humanity. It will also teach us that brotherhood and peace can be established only on the basis of the spiritual experience of the Oneness of life and existence, and of the fundamental divinity of man.

Let me cite a few experiences of that great personality, Sri Ramakrishna. When he was a little boy about five or six years old, he was going to visit a temple. On the way, a beautiful scene—a deep speck of cloud with a number of cranes flying in front of it—made him realize God-consciousness. Beauty, the *Sundara* aspect of the Divine, transported him and gave him divine joy. That was the first experience of this hero in the spiritual realm. Later on, when on various occasions he would take the rôles of different religious personalities in country dramas, plays, or games, he would actually enter into a spiritual consciousness. Perhaps you will be surprised to know that our children in India, even today, have their dolls and games associated with the divine incarnations or with different personal aspects of God. Our dolls are the images or statues of divine incarnations. This boy, already a leader among his associates, in play would actually identify himself with the divine personalities he impersonated and would remain wholly oblivious of the external world and the sense experiences of life, and for hours at a time would remain absorbed in those states of consciousness. During his childhood he would often retire to the woods leaving his playmates and remain absorbed in meditation and communion with God.

Later on, when he was about seventeen or eighteen years old, he went to Calcutta and lived there for a number of years. This is the time when he began scientifically and rationally to experience God. Please remember that I have some very definite justification for using the word "scientifically." Sri Ramakrishna's faith brought out his divine love, which we know occurred also in the lives of Saint Thomas, Saint Theresa, Saint Francis of Assisi, Saint John of the Cross and of other great spiritual leaders belonging to various religions. For some years Sri Ramakrishna did not pursue any method systematically under any religious teacher, but followed his own inner urge.

It was when he was employed as a priest in the Temple of

Dakshineswar that he was completely convinced that he must himself directly experience God, the Mother of the Universe, whom his heart desired so much to see. In the course of worship, he used to cry to the Divine Mother to appear to him and visibly accept all the offerings. Desire for communion with the Divine Mother seized his whole consciousness. It became gradually impossible for him to observe the formalities of worship; so he applied himself day and night wholly to obtaining a direct experience of God. He went through untold pangs of agony till he attained that divine realization. One day when he became almost desperate for the sight of God, the Divine Mother, he obtained a unique realization of God. That wonderful day the Divine Mother appeared to him first as a personal God; then, the whole phenomenal world vanished, the doors, buildings, everything vanished. There remained only a flood of light, a flood of consciousness, a flood of bliss. He stayed in that state for a long time.

After this he underwent religious discipline by going through the different spiritual practices prescribed by the various schools of Hindu thought. In India we have made a science of religious practices and experiences. We have distinct methods by which different types of persons, according to their inner tendencies and individual feeling of relationship with God, can scientifically and rationally reach God-consciousness. The science of devotion recognizes that different individuals have strong feelings of love for certain persons in the family: father, mother, brother, friend or children. Psychologically we all have a spontaneous, intimate and strong feeling toward any one of them. Hindu teachers understand that devotion can grow very effectively if any one of these relationships is established with God. The innate strong emotions can then easily be directed toward God so that no mental energy will be lost. Devotional life becomes natural and easy when the course of love is directed towards the Divine Mother, Divine Father, Divine Friend or Divine Child.

Sri Ramakrishna wanted to verify the different religious methods meant for people of various characters to see whether every method was effective or not. Of course these methods were prescribed by the Scriptures and by other personalities, yet they were not from his own experiences. He would often say to himself, "Why should I be narrow and one-sided? I must find and enjoy God in various ways through various methods." Consequently, with the help of expert teachers, he went through all the different methods.

The first real teacher that Sri Ramakrishna had was a lady who taught him the mysteries of the various spiritual practices prescribed by the Hindu systems. Successively, as if he were different persons with different characteristics, he looked upon God first as his mother, then as his father, his master, his child, his friend, etc., remaining wholly absorbed in one attitude till he reached the highest realization by that particular method. He found that every one of these ways led him to the same spiritual realization and God-consciousness. He then wanted to verify the teachings, experiences and methods of other religions. One after another, he systematically followed Christianity, Mohammedanism and other religious systems under the direction of expert teachers of every particular school of thought, and reached the same goal.

One peculiarity we observe in his life is that when he followed any one system, he would identify himself with that religion thoroughly—and he was a thorough man in every sense of the term. When he practiced Christianity, he was a thoroughgoing Christian; and after realizing Christ and God-consciousness through Christ, he turned wholly to another method. He was not an eclectic, choosing a bit here and there from one system and another. Gradually he went through all the various phases of the different religions.

He then came to another state, the experience of the Impersonal God, God without form, without attribute. There came a Hindu monk who taught him the system of this realization. You will be surprised to know that this monk himself admitted that his student realized the same state of consciousness in the course of three days' practice that had taken him forty long years to realize. The teacher himself, marvelling at the realization and experience of the great disciple, remained with him for more than six months, against his vowed custom, actually to learn the very wonderful fact that God is not merely impersonal but is also personal. God is not merely a continual reality, but God can be experienced also in His personal aspect. The Relative (*Maya*) is not non-existence. Both *Nitya* and *Lila*, Eternal and Phenomenal, are phases of the Absolute. Both Impersonal and Personal are true at different stages of spiritual realization and can be experienced.

From the life of Sri Ramakrishna, we find that mystic experiences are not mysterious entities or hallucinations. It has been a common mistake all over the world for so many centuries to think when you meet a man of God, a man who has direct experience of God, that he is peculiar or has hallucinations. You would perhaps try to send him to an insane asylum. All the great spiritual leaders of the world were suspected of being mental cases. Let me cite the experience of Saint Theresa when she was actually accused of insanity and of being possessed by the devil. She herself declared to the world, "the result of mere operations of the imagination is but to weaken the soul . . . whereas a genuine heavenly vision yields to her a harvest of ineffable spiritual riches, and an admirable renewal of bodily strength. I alleged these reasons to those who so often accused my visions of being the work of the enemy of mankind and the sport of my imagination . . . I showed them the jewels which the divine hand had left with me:—they were my actual dispositions." She then tells us, "If the demon were its author, he could not have used, in order to lose me and lead me to hell, an expedient so contrary to his own interests as that of uprooting my vices." She was a transformed personality. From the life of Sri Ramakrishna, we fully realize that mystic experiences do not make us insane but make us better men and women. They illumine and make us pure, unselfish, loving and humble and efface our egotism.

I told you that Sri Ramakrishna scientifically followed the methods of God-realization. Thereby I mean that he systematically followed the methods of different religions and actually left scientific records of the experiences for us also to go through in order to realize God. In the scientific world we find a tendency not to accept anything unless the facts are actually proven to us. You will not believe anything, you will not take anything for granted. Sri Ramakrishna was a man of that type. He was, in fact, a product of this modern age. He would not accept even God-consciousness until he had himself verified it, until he had realized the fact. He would not accept anything whether given him by a Hindu, Christian or Mohammedan teacher. He tested it first as you and I test the different facts of science by our own experiments. Only then did he accept. Consequently, as a leader of the scientific world, he shows us that God-consciousness is not a matter of intellectual discussion nor of the father-transference of Western psychology, nor limited to rituals and ceremonies, nor to books and Scriptures, but that God-consciousness is to be experienced in our lives.

About two thousand years ago, some Orientals idealized the life of Christ, and about twenty-six centuries ago a few others idealized the life of Buddha. You may feel that these great ones were dreamers, that they have no value in our lives, in our scientific world. Many of the foremost thinkers of the scientific school consider the spiritual experiences of Jesus, Buddha, Ramakrishna and other great spiritual personalities as cases of self-hypnosis, delusion, and hallucination.

Today there is a wave of psychological interest. Everyone in America, at least every thinking person, puts tremendous value upon the study of psychology. Why? Because we all realize that psychology works. Psychology gives something to our everyday life. Psychology regulates the use of the mind that we may influence other minds. We can influence others in various ways. Consequently, particularly in America, people are placing great store upon the study of psychology. It is true that modern psychology, which has been developed very much in Europe and in America, is giving us something which we did not have before. The concrete use of mind was not achieved until a few years ago. Modern psychology, in spite of its defects, narrowness and incompleteness, has done a great deal so far as our practical life is concerned. You go to a department store. All sales men and women use psychology so that they can play with the minds of others. Wherever you go, you find the effects of the study of psychology. You go to a doctor, and he will tell you that without the understanding of psychology he cannot cure many ailments. You go to a psychoanalyst, and he will try to discover your complexes and help you accordingly.

What do the psychologists say about the spiritual experiences and life of Sri Ramakrishna? Suppose we present his experiences to the modern psychologists: I am sure that in Europe and America, perhaps with the exception of one or two, they will declare that this man had hallucinations, that the experiences he used to have about God were nothing but self-hypnosis, delusion, epilepsy or some other form of mental disturbance. Most modern psychologists assume that the "idea of God" is due to childhood dependence on the father. God is nothing but "father-transference" to overcome fear and other weaknesses. The Behaviorists go a step further and want to eliminate the idea of God from human life. Some psychoanalysts dogmatically give even obnoxious and shocking theories regarding the idea of God. A few years ago, one of my best friends in America had occasion to talk to one of the greatest psychiatrists of New England. He is usually consulted in serious cases. When my friend spoke of religious problems, the psychologist suggested that these were just foolish ideas of man, that at times man adopts these religious ideas either to console his mind or to get a little encouragement and strength from the fictitious idea of God. Many psychologists will actually look down upon you if you talk of religion or of God, and will think you peculiar. I know what my friend thought when, with so many things to discuss, she met the psychologist who asked, "Do you have any visions or experiences?" He wanted to establish another pathological case based on one of his pet theories.

Let us evaluate the experiences of the great mystics and also the experiences of the great psychologists, and let us find which are scientific in the religious field and which are not. All the great spiritual leaders and spiritual personalities, such as Sri

Ramakrishna, were sometime or other regarded by the common run of folk as men of hallucination or as insane persons. Why? Because they were unusual; because their experiences were not the experiences of psychologists and other ordinary people living on the sense plane. After all, what does the psychologist study? Until a few years ago, psychologists were limited to the conscious activities of the mind, to just the surface of the mind, and nothing more than that. Only of late, just for twenty-five or thirty years, a few psychologists have been talking of the subconscious mind and describing something as subconscious, and even here their general conclusions are very vague, insufficient and incomplete. The methods of their study are not yet thorough and convincing.

One of the greatest psychologists of the modern world, Dr. Jung in his *Modern Man in Search of a Soul*, tells us, without the least shade of doubt, after so many years of study and of experimentation, after many years of medical and pathological practice, that Western psychology is a beginner's attempt in comparison with the Oriental system of Yoga, particularly of the Hindu system of Yoga. He understands the validity of spiritual realization and experiences. Similar statements are made by other profound thinkers, such as Dr. William Brown of London, who does not discard religion and studies the subject thoroughly and not from a narrow point of view. Of late, fortunately, Dr. Alexis Carrell is shedding new light for the West on spiritual experiences. He tells us emphatically, in his *Man the Unknown*, that spiritual experiences are valid; moreover that man's life and experience is incomplete without them. It was here, right here in America, that one of the greatest psychologists of the West did not decry spiritual experiences, mystic realizations, as mere facts of pathology and hallucination. It was in Boston that Professor William James, in his *Varieties of Religious Experience*, did not discard these experiences as pathological, although he did not have a final understanding because, as he admitted, he did not have a complete understanding of the mind nor had he followed spiritual practices. But he was not a narrow person, and he presented to us without any prejudice certain facts for psychologists and scientific thinkers to judge and evaluate. He discussed and presented not only the experiences and methods of the Christian mystics, but also those of the Hindu, Mohammedan and other mystics.

I do not deny that there are many pathological cases that assume religious ideas. Many insane persons are in the business world, in banking or commercial fields. Others are managing factories, or rather manage factories and then become insane. They may be obsessed by some particular idea and lose balance. Does that mean that your banking or commercial ways of living make people insane? Would you discard your banking system because such and such a person became insane while being a bank president? You might meet some persons who have an extreme form of hallucination regarding money, friendship or something else. There are persons who actually think so many foolish things and do so many destructive acts in the name of friendship, in the name of love and in the name of so many other beautiful tendencies of man. Would you say that friendship is the cause of insanity or that love is the root of insanity? If any scientist or any psychologist concludes that religion produces insanity, he is certainly narrow and unscientific. He is concluding more than is warranted by the partial facts. He is not following the proper methods of investigation and generalization.

Psychologists try to measure spiritual experiences by methods applicable to other sciences. Different scientific studies are to be followed through various methods. For instance, you do not apply the same method of study to psychology as to physics. Similarly, mystic realization or spiritual experience has its own individual method. If by following these prescribed methods systematically and exactly you fail to realize the truth, then, and only then, can you legitimately conclude that God is meaningless, that He is a mere father-transference, a fictitious idea created by weak persons to have a feeling of shelter and solace in their troubles. Many modern psychologists are committing this great blunder when they generalize and actually look down upon all spiritual experiences or ignore the higher mental and spiritual states.

Now, how will the experiences of Sri Ramakrishna be regarded by Western psychologists? They only study a few conscious activities or perhaps get a glimpse of some of the subconscious tendencies. Sri Ramakrishna's life and experiences, as they belong to the superconscious, open up a new realm of psychology. Modern psychologists have not even the slightest idea of that realm. Consequently, they will conclude that these experiences of Sri Ramakrishna are hallucinations. Spiritual experiences illumine the whole mind, and lead us to a state where we transcend the limitations of time, space and causation. We transcend the limitations of name and form. We transcend the limitations of the phenomenal world. It is true that very few persons have these unusual and extraordinary experiences, but, nevertheless, those who have them find them to be more valid than ordinary phenomenal experiences. You will all agree with me that today you think about certain things in one way, and the next day you change your ideas. Your emotional reactions constantly vary. Today you think that certain persons are wonderful, and tomorrow your mind changes and you discard that idea about them. This is because you have not the deeper understanding of them. We have only superficial understanding from external expressions, which may have different inner causes. For instance, a gift may be made to another by reason of different inner urges: love, feeling of service, greed, expectation, spite. You may love the person, so you give, or you may feel that the person is in need, or you may give to the person in service or worship of God. You may again give something in expectation of receiving something in return. You may give to make another jealous, or because of being angry with another, or in spite and so on. When modern psychologists try to study the unconscious mind, they really grope in the dark. Although they may sometimes hit upon the right unconscious motive or urge, yet their understanding of the unconscious is often very unsatisfactory, incomplete and vague. Their research is based purely on the objective study of the mind and is often coloured by preconceived notions of the nature of urges and contents of the unconscious. But a man of higher unfoldment or of mystic realization has complete understanding of every fact, of every person. He sees through your body and mind the reality behind you. He deals with the inner region, the inner man! None but a man of spiritual realization can give us the total experience of man's existence. By virtue of his own inner illumination, he has the penetrating understanding of the inner nature of others.

The life and experiences of Sri Ramakrishna take us very far away from modern psychology, psychoanalysis or experimental psychology. A new study is required. If we want to develop a complete psychology, we have to discipline ourselves first. We have first to have superconscious realization and experiences. Then alone shall we be in a position to give the world a complete psychology. Until you can discipline your mind, and train yourself wholly and completely, you have no access to the mystic experiences of the superconscious realm. Until you take up the methods that will lead you to mystic realization, you have not the slightest idea of the existence of superconscious realization nor of its effect.

The Yoga systems of India give us a deeper understanding of the complete mind: subconscious, conscious and superconscious. It is true that Yogis present the life of Sri Ramakrishna as an actual demonstration of the highest form of psychology. If you want to study the complete and total field of man's mind, you have to interpret and study in the light of the experiences of the type of this great man. I am not asking you to accept him or any one else, nor am I asking you to present him to the world without verifying his experiences. Sri Ramakrishna himself tells us, "Come along, have the experiences." You all know that when Swami Vivekananda, his great disciple who was the lion of the Parliament of Religions at Chicago in 1893, challenged him with the question, "Have you seen God?" Sri Ramakrishna answered, "Yes. I have seen Him and I can show Him to you." That was the declaration made not only to Swami Vivekananda, but to the whole world, to you and to me. Yes, a man can experience God, and that man can also show you God. Sri Ramakrishna not only had superconscious experiences but also knew the methods and taught them to his disciples. This knowledge can be given to others. There is no exclusive idea about this. I saw many of the disciples of this great master who had had superconscious experiences. Their love, unselfishness, purity and other wonderful qualities proved to me without the least shade of doubt that superconscious realizations were valid, practical, dynamic and can also be demonstrated.

I have presented to you the one personality who lived the life of a Hindu, a Christian, a Mohammedan, a Buddhist and a Jew and realized the truth by following different methods. Consequently, we are totally convinced that even today God can be experienced and realized by any person, regardless of his church affiliation or religious creed. The only thing that is required is intense love for that realization and the strong urge to realize God. Since we are all born in this age and have consciously or unconsciously imbibed scientific tendencies, let us be thoroughly scientific and make a worthwhile experiment on the realization of God or on spiritual experiences. Let us also find that God is true, in our own inner consciousness, in our own everyday life, in our own actions and thoughts. We shall then find that God-consciousness will unite us, will make us serve the veritable expressions of God as so many human forms.

Sri Ramakrishna's realizations were not static but dynamic. He went out with his intense love to serve the veritable expressions of God in human and other forms, because he realized that the Infinite was not only present in a few persons but also was present in all beings, even in plants and in inanimate objects. This is a very significant fact and is the practical solution of our modern problems.

The mystic experiences of Sri Ramakrishna did not make him lose what he possessed before, but made him more efficient, practical, methodical, systematic and intelligent. A new vista was moreover open to him. He gained an immediate and direct knowledge of a new realm previously unknown to him or to others. His joy and peace knew no bounds. Above all, mystic experiences made him love his disciples and all persons with whom he came in contact, nay, all beings.

Let me present a few instances and facts to modern psychologists and to others for their consideration. One day, hard stones were thrown down on green blades of grass. Sri Ramakrishna, without knowing what was going on, called out, "Oh my, they are beating me, they are pressing my heart, they are crushing my chest!" On inquiry it was found that some people were treating the tender blades of growing grass ruthlessly. When they desisted, his pain stopped. Once, at a distance, out of sight of Sri Ramakrishna and unknown to him, a bullock was severely beaten. Scars of assault appeared on the back of Sri Ramakrishna without his knowing the cause. Another time two boatmen were quarreling and came to blows. Sri Ramakrishna felt those blows on his own person.

Would the psychologists believe these facts? I ask the psychologists this question: how did these things happen? You could not say that they were hallucinations. You could not say that this man's mind was wrong. You could not say that this was a case of auto-suggestion or of self-hypnosis. It was that this mystic had identified himself completely with the whole of existence, with the whole realm of reality. Consequently, he felt the fighting of the men, the beating of the bullock and maltreating of the grass keenly within himself. This is possible only when a man unites himself with the source of existence, with the source of life.

When a man realizes the Oneness of life and existence, then alone does he feel thus. Is not this wonderful love? If the mystic experiences of Sri Ramakrishna can make him love even blades of grass, effectively not sentimentally, I would certainly not only worship him, but I would also crave to become as close as possible to that life. Is not this experience worth while? Would you call a man of that experience a pathological case? I wish we were all of that type. I wish we could all attain even one hundredth part of that Oneness. Then our maladies, our sufferings, our hateful and destructive tendencies would vanish in no time. This world would be a place of joy and peace, of harmony and synthesis.

Mystic realizations make you the source of love, the source of peace. Real spiritual realizations will unite you with the

whole of existence, with the whole of reality. In fact, superconscious realizations are really the background and dynamic
forces of unselfish work and social justice. This the real basis of
Sri Ramakrishna's humanism. Modern humanists forget the real
place of man and isolate him from God—the Real Existence,
the background. Some are atheistical and the rest are agnostic
and find no need for God. Their incentives and motives are not
deep enough to convince the minds of men and to induce them
to carry on humanitarian activities. Sri Ramakrishna's experiences furnish the real background of social work. He shows
that the work should be done in the spirit of service and worship. Then the work performed by the aspirant will lead him to
the highest realization of Truth. Of course a man of spiritual
unfoldment himself does humanitarian work, being already established in the knowledge of the Oneness of life, while the aspirant works to gain that realization. The Great Master one day
emphasized to his disciples in the course of conversation, "not
compassion for man, but service to man." He emphasized that
we are to regard man as the veritable embodiment of God,
Narayana.

Man has greed, injustice and selfishness because he feels he
must look after his own interest and the interest of his own
family. Selfishness is the basis of all troubles in the family,
among nations and in internal affairs. All claims of exclusive
rights and privileges are also due to selfishness. A man of superconscious realization removes all barriers of selfishness from his
life because he feels in all the presence of God, the All-loving
Being. As a result, such a man serves every one as the veritable
expression of God. A man of such spiritual unfoldment is an
object lesson to all. His very life and actions make others unselfish and inspire them to give love and service to God and man.
Such a life is, therefore, of great pragmatic value to the world
apart from the personal joy and happiness afforded to the mystic himself.

If you want to verify these experiences, you must identify
yourself with the Oneness of existence. Then alone are you in
a position to evaluate, and then alone can you effectively help

and serve others. You will then be a source of power, inspiration and love. Your human relations will be enjoyable and uplifting.

So, my friends, I implore you to assimilate that life. Then you will understand the experiences of Jesus, Buddha, Saint Francis, Saint Paul, Swami Vivekananda, and many others. You will also understand that the different religious methods are true and are leading different types of men to God. Finally, you will realize the inner divinity of all, and thereby you will change your attitude and behavior to others and influence them effectively to do the same. Let us do it right now. We have heard the clarion call that you and I can have that realization which Sri Ramakrishna had. Let us make our lives blessed by realizing the Truth, by realizing God, by identifying ourselves with the Oneness of life and existence.

REMINISCENCES

SWAMI ASESHANANDA

I am thankful to Swami Akhilananda for his valued friendship and wise counsel, which helped me relinquish some of my dreamy ideas about the supreme purpose of life. Akhilananda, in a sense, has awakened me from the slumber of dogmatic patriotism. At that time I was closely associated with a group which preached to me the idea that salvation of the country from the British yoke was more important than the salvation of the soul from the fetters of the world. Some of its members spoke vehemently against monastic life as a symbol of life-negation and escapism. To think of mukti or freedom of one's own soul while so many people in the world were in agony and affliction was a selfish thing. They would quote to me poet Rabindranath Tagore's words, "To attain liberation through renunciation is not the path that I choose to follow." Because they were highly intellectual people and good moralists, I was very much influenced by their thoughts and ideas. Swami Akhilananda would quote to me the significant passage from the Upanishads to counteract their ideas—"Not by work, nor by wealth, nor by progeny, but by renunciation alone is immortality to be attained." But all in vain!

Then one day Swami Akhilananda said to me, "It is not possible for me to convince you. I am not a monk, although I hope to be so one day. Only he who lives a monastic life in letter and spirit can convince others. Let us go to Maharaj, an ideal monk and a spiritual son of Sri Ramakrishna, the great world-teacher born in our times." A day was fixed. Swami Akhilananda and I rode the street-car up to Shyambazar. Then we walked together and arrived at Balaram Bose's house at Baghbazar. Swami Brahmananda was in his small room rapt in his thoughts. After some time we were permitted to go in and salute Maharaj. Swami Akhilananda introduced me, saying "This is my friend, Kiran. We study in the same college. We live in the same dormitory. He is a junior to me by one year. He is a good boy. He wants to talk to you. Please bless him." Maharaj glanced at me with his glowing, penetrating eyes and he said, "You are Nirode's friend, good. Come another day. I am not feeling well today." Many times I met Maharaj but the date of personal interview was postponed. Probably he was testing my earnestness and sincerity. At last Maharaj spoke to me. He said in a soft voice with a ring of authority: "Practice truthfulness. Practice brahmacharya—continence of thought, word and deed. That is the way to attain the vision of God and be satisfied forever." There was something behind those words—a power—a presence which penetrated into my heart and made me say to myself, "That is the ideal I will live for and struggle unceasingly to implement into action in my own life. May He bless me."

Swami Akhilananda joined the Ramakrishna Order at the Bhubaneswar Monastery in 1919. Through his encouragement and loving persuasion, I joined the Belur Monastery in 1921. Maharaj later sent Akhilananda to Madras Monastery after a few months of his stay at the Bhubaneswar Math, where he had the opportunity of serving his beloved guru. Akhilananda drew his inspiration from the words of wisdom that came from the lips of Swami Brahmananda. I too gathered a strong impetus to live a life of truthfulness by associating with Swami Brahmananda, an illumined soul of profound experience, when he stayed at the Belur Math.

Sri Ramakrishna used to say, "If you sit by a fire, you are bound to get warmth. Likewise, if you associate with an illumined soul, you are sure to get spiritual development and inner contentment. That contentment was felt by me when I heard from the lips of Maharaj after morning meditation, with the dawn approaching and Ganges flowing by, and Maharaj seated calmly at the Belur Math: "Pray to the Lord with a longing heart. Tell Him freely that you desire Him and Him alone.

Don't doubt that He exists. Those who are lowly and humble are soon blessed with His vision. If you approach Him with sincere faith, He will surely reveal Himself to you. Do not feel shy because you have made some mistakes or have not called on Him for a long time. He is the very embodiment of forgiveness. He is the very soul of compassion. He cares little for man's faults. Go to Him with the simplicity of a child. He will receive you like a father receives his dear son. Be simple and guileless. Without simplicity and childlike faith, nobody can realize Him."

Another incident comes to my memory. That day Maharaj spoke, laying special emphasis on work. He said, "Always remember that through work you are worshipping the Lord. One can see Him with the eye of devotion. If you work with the idea of pleasing men, you will be disappointed. You can find peace and joy only if you can remember the Lord. If He is pleased, the world is pleased. In favourable or in adverse circumstances feel that you have none but Him and that you are serving Him through the faithful performance of your allotted duties."

After our Brahmacharya initiation Maharaj left Belur Math and went to Calcutta. I would visit him there at Balaram Mandir. Almost the last words of Maharaj were: "My children, cling to God. He will be with you always. Work, devotion, discrimination—each one is a path to attain union with God. With the same whole-hearted devotion with which a devotee worships the Lord in the Shrine, he must serve the Lord in the poor, in the sick, in the lowly. Who are you to help another? It is only when the Lord gives you the power that you can really serve. Every Jiva is really Shiva—a manifestation of God."

What comes foremost in my mind when I reflect on the benefit that I have derived from my long association with Swami Akhilananda is the idea of Guru-bhakti or devotion to the Guru. Faith in the Guru was the power behind all his activities which prompted him to undertake any responsibility, however difficult, and carry it out to its legitimate fulfillment. The Upanishad says:

Can a man roll up the sky
Like a piece of skin?
Can a man end his misery
Without the realization of God?

If the truths of the scriptures are meditated upon by a man in the highest degree, devoted to God and to his guru as to his God, they will shine forth, verily they will shine forth.

I believe it is due to the unwavering faith in his guru, the spiritual teacher, that Akhilananda could achieve so much influence in the West. When I saw him in Boston in 1947 he radiated nothing but sweetness and love. He was a competent teacher, friend, and guide to many Western people who sought his help, coming from different walks of life. He was a good cook also. He not only prepared delicious dishes with his own hand, he also ministered to the spiritual hunger of man and served food to satisfy the appetite of the soul. He gave comfort and peace to many a broken heart. He spoke not so much from the intellect but from the inner recess of his soul. That is the reason why his instructions are so appealing and practical. May *Spiritual Practices* written by my friend Akhilananda be a guide-book towards spiritual growth in Europe and America and be a lever to forge better understanding between the East and the West.

Portland, Oregon

❀

PETER A. BERTOCCI

Swami Akhilananda on several occasions was a dinner guest in our home. Mrs. Bertocci, our three sons, and I bowed our heads in prayer as Swami at our request said grace. There was a brief silence, and the Swami intoned: "Om!"—and immediately took our nerves and minds with him to another dimension of Being. "Oh God, who art our Father; Oh God, who art our Mother!"—once more he broke through our stereotypes, and yet he used symbols of a special tie we had with each other and with the universal One.

Symbol? Symbol that forced us to *be* and yet *express*; to be beyond every action! That was Swami's witness amongst us, in our home, in our community and country, beyond his Centers in Boston and Providence, and in the services and social occasions where his beaming countenance and reaching-demeanor always created a peace-beyond-comfort. Further testimony to these characteristics of Swami came from students who, disenchanted with their own religious upbringing, returned from the counselor to whom I had sent them. He had a way of touching people that was not an "encounter" but a new introduction to what he would have called their deepest selves.

I have often referred to the Swami in my classes as a missionary from India, and its basic Hindu tradition, to America. And, as I have noticed of good Christian missionaries to India, he became as one of us. With a quiet forcefulness, he pointed out that so much in our Judeo-Christian and "Western" heritage was not at odds with the spiritual and cultural heritage that was his. He helped us to see what was more universal in us and our "realities" by taking us always beyond the vulgar "commonplaces" in our experience. His spoken and written meditations became more meaningful to us because he reached beyond the immediate differences among psychologies, theologies, and philosophies—and never just to win a point!

Many of us—for whom this life was sometimes a song, sometimes a poem, and always saintly—see Swami's presence among us beautifully symbolized by what he insisted on doing "by himself" at dinners honoring the memory of Sri Ramakrishna. Were there fifty or a hundred and fifty, he came to each place and each person with the curry he himself had prepared, to offer an additional helping. For him we were individuals—to be served with a grace and dignity that was Swami's expression of the One.

Boston University
Boston, Massachusetts

BETTY A. BOGERT

"When you go to visit a lawyer, what kind of thoughts come into your mind? Thoughts about legal matters. With a doctor, you think about sickness and medicine. These thoughts come to you because the person you are with at the moment is living in that particular atmosphere. So also with a holy man. You may not know anything about him, but this is the test: when you come into his presence, the thought of God will come to you—even though the holy man may be talking of something quite different." Thus spoke Swami Prabhavananda in commenting on Jesus' words, "Ye are the light of the world..."[1]

Swami Akhilananda more than met this test, quite unbeknownst to him, as I happened to sit beside him at a meeting of the Society for the Scientific Study of Religion in the early 1960's at Yale University. I knew almost nothing about him. He spoke little. Yet he radiated such unique and transforming power that this one encounter left an indelible impression.

Were I to attempt to paint his portrait, his almost transparent body could not get in the way of his gentle and penetrating person. From within, would glow a quiet effulgence which might overcome a sensitive spirit and yet be completely missed by others less sensitive.

Were I asked the question, "What influence persuaded you in the direction of seeking God along the personal path of spiritual enlightenment for yourself and others?", I would point to the mysterious power in the spirit of Swami Akhilananda, whose light shines eternally in the lives of many.

Lisbon, New Hampshire

---

[1] In *The Sermon on the Mount According to Vedanta*, Mentor Books (New York: New American Library, 1963).

EDWIN P. BOOTH

" What is man that Thou art mindful of him, or the son of man that Thou visitest him? For Thou hast made him but little lower than the angels, and hast crowned him with glory and honor."

This program is called "We Believe."[1]

I try to say to myself each morning, as it is my privilege to come to it, what it is that I am talking about this morning that we believe. There is a sentence in our Christian tradition that God has not left himself without a witness at any time. And it is about that that I believe this morning. I believe that God has not left himself without a witness, and that the Christian witness is, perhaps, one of many witnesses which God has authenticated in history.

I wish to pay my tribute, therefore, this morning, to a witness to the Eternal that comes out of a tradition not my own. This is out of the great tradition of the East, from India. Now long ago when the Indian peoples were struggling, as all other peoples of earth struggle through to self-consciousness and to a realization of the existence of God and of our ability to talk to him, there arose in Indian thought a great tradition, similar to that in Hebraic thought in our Jewish-Christian tradition. The Old Testament is a collection of many concepts, many ideas, many insights into history. Well, the Indian people have such a collection too. They have over many centuries had men of keen minds, gentle hearts, skillful social programs. And the gathering of the thinking of these men is brought together in the great scriptures of Hinduism. And as Hinduism cuts itself down to its various subdivisions just exactly as Christianity does, one of them emerges as Buddhism. Buddha was a great and kindly teacher. But Buddhism too must subdivide itself. Now we must be very patient with a religion not our own,

---

[1] This talk was given March 18, 1960 on "We Believe" over Station WHDH-TV, Boston.

because the vocabulary, the overtones of our experiences, are apt to move in and color our understandings when they should not do so. The man who has a religion has the right to tell us what it means. And so, as we Christians survey the subdivisions of Christianity in all its Catholic branches and all its Protestant branches, we ought to be very kindly disposed as we survey the subdivisions of the mighty Indian faiths also.

One of the subdivisions under the Hindu-Buddha break-down into particularizations is called in our time the Vedanta Society. There is a meeting of the Vedanta Society, there is a gathering of people believing in this understanding of the ways of God, in Boston, and one in Providence, Rhode Island. For thirty years now, I have personally known the leader of one of the Vedanta Society groups, the one settled in Boston and working jointly with the one in Providence. Vedanta, by the way, means a school of interpretation, so that a Vedanta Society can arise within the great tradition of the Eastern faiths, and this is what has happened.

And the Society to which I refer now has arisen out of the following of the teachings of an Indian named Sri Ramakrishna. Sri Ramakrishna was born in 1836 and died in 1886, so it is a very modern movement. There is representing the Sri Rama-krishna Vedanta Society in Boston a Swami whom many of us have learned to love. "Swami" is a reverential title in that cultural area, such as "The Reverend" is in ours. If we say to ourselves "The Reverend Mr. Jones," we would say in their tradition "The Swami Mr. Jones." Now the Swami who bears witness in our American Christian society for the deep intensities of the spiritual life is named Akhilananda, Swami Akhilananda. All the Swamis in the Sri Ramakrishna movement have *ananda* as the closing syllables of their name. This means "the blessed" —Akhil the blessed, Swami Akhilananda. There was the Swami Vivekananda, and the Swami Akhandananda.

This is a strange thing now; let us be quiet for a moment and consider what our Christian tradition has been like. We have sent our testifiers to India for many, many years. One of my mother's great-uncles was the first missionary of the Church

156

of Scotland to India. And a hundred years ago he wrote a book on the development of his mission in that distant field. And now I sit in Boston and bear tribute to the reverse, to the validity and the value of a missionary from the Hindu tradition, from India, to us in our society here. What a marvelous thing it is for us to build bridges between our faiths! If we really believe that God has not left himself without a witness in any land or any people, then how warmly we must welcome the quiet, gentle testimonies steadily maintained in our fast-moving society by a quiet man from India who speaks the language of peace and gentleness.

It is said, though I'm not sure I feel the full force of it, but all the great leaders we have in this field say it to us and so I must give it consideration, that India knows more about peace than we Westerners do; that we Westerners are vigorous, aggressive. Well, vigorous and aggressive we are. We know this. And we are affirmative, too affirmative of late. And that long before we had a culture in the West, in that mighty peninsula we call India that juts down from the Himalaya mountains to the north and is flanked by the mighty waters until it reaches its peak in the south, that there was developed in this subcontinent of Asia, as we like to call it, a conception of the Eternal which is more quiet than ours. They seem to feel that spiritual life is all around them, that this temporary physical life you and I experience here is a phase of our evolution; that our spirits belong to the Great Spirit, yea, will be absorbed in it finally; and that through the long course of human history, maybe our spirits have had lives in other forms and at other times.

It is highly ethical, this concept, because one advances, according to my friend Swami Akhilananda and others, one advances from one level of life to another according to the goodness of his life, according to the ethical quality of his life. They call this *dharma*, we call this ethics: to obey what is commanded; to bear what must be borne; to speak in quietness; to view with honor and affection God's creatures other than his human creatures; to see all of life as a mighty spiritual movement of which this physical part we now endure is perhaps transitory and passing; to rest oneself, so to speak, back on an eternal ocean of peace.

Swami Akhilananda was won into this concept of Sri Ramakrishna's understanding of ancient Hinduism. Sri Ramakrishna was a priest of the goddess Kali. This Hinduism is basically one in its idea of God. It is hard for us Westerners to understand this, but it is one. But the one is broken into many appreciations, as our Western world is, too. And Sri Ramakrishna was a priest of one of the particularizations of the divine life, namely Kali. The Swami Akhilananda was won into the fellowship of Sri Ramakrishna's group when he was a young boy. He never dreamed of being a teacher or a preacher. All he wanted to do was to be a cook in the society of the Brothers of Sri Ramakrishna, that he could know their peace and understand their friendship. Well, the little lad that long ago wanted to be a cook in the Brothers of Sri Ramakrishna has now for thirty years magnificently defended in Providence and Boston, in Brown University and Boston University, in Massachusetts Institute of Technology and Harvard College, the faith he loves. This is a remarkable story. Swami Akhilananda has gathered us together once a year at a dinner meeting in honor of the Holy Mother of his faith. And we have sat, we, the inheritors of the Western tradition, quietly as he and his friends explained to us the mighty Mother-principle of his Indian God-concept, as we have explained to him the mighty Father-principle of our Western God-concept.

It is interesting always to know him. He is a marvelous person. He does not live according to the customs of the East, for he speaks peace to us of the West, so he lives according to our customs. He has a good home, he wears our Western clothes, he drives a big good Western automobile. But everywhere he goes, his smiling face, his quiet word, his gentle hand, is a blessing of peace to all of us. I was ill once, quite seriously, a few years ago. He stepped into my hospital room on several occasions, and quietly, out of the ancient East, I heard his words: "Peace, peace, peace." Well, it is marvelous to know that the religions communicate to each other through living individuals, warm and gentle, quiet and patient.

I give you the Swami Akhilananda's word, peace.

Sri Ramakrishna said: "If you will seek for God, seek him in man."

※

RALPH WENDELL BURHOE

I knew Swami Akhilananda during his last ten years, working with him or meeting him in connection with several different groups in the Boston area that were concerned with religion and the intellectual life. When I had offices at the Massachusetts Institute of Technology I often met him in the corridors on his way to ministering to students. We worked together in the development of the Institute on Religion in an Age of Science, which was a group of a few hundred persons at most, many of them distinguished scientists, others scholars, clergymen, and interested persons from many professions and business activities. But I knew him in connection with a number of other groups as well.

What impressed me was his goodness and the respect many held for him as a person. His own respect for and kindly helpfulness to others, together with his basic confidence in a transhuman wisdom and power guiding human destiny in the end, made him a beloved friend and healing spirit. His wisdom was a wisdom for living that was ingrained in his behavior. His gentleness and humility seemed to be part of an incarnated wisdom that operated as it were automatically in his behavior.

He was important as a contributor to the development of the Institute on Religion in an Age of Science because he was so familiar with two major religious cultures: the Christianity of the West and the Hinduism of the East. He seemed to have a natural and almost instinctive tendency to translate from one to the other, back and forth. But he was also especially concerned with the sciences and the implications of the sciences for religion. I found him interested in the whole range of the sciences from the physical to the psychosocial and their implications for human values and religion. We enjoyed talking about these matters on many occasions, often with others from the disciplines of religious studies or the sciences. He became, with a few dozen others, a member of the Advisory Board of IRAS, and a faithful participant in and contributor to its annual conferences during a midsummer week on Star Island (ten miles out in the Atlantic Ocean from Portsmouth, New Hampshire) as well as to its smaller occasional meetings in the neighborhood of Boston during the 1950's and until his death.

One bit of synthesis of religion and science in which we shared a good deal in our developing thought was concerned with the problem of the meaning of human life in view of the fact of the inevitable death of all living bodies. We early concluded that the Hindu doctrines of reincarnation were psychologically equivalent to the Christian doctrines of resurrection (or the alternative doctrine of the immortal soul). We further shared the view that the evolutionary pictures of the sciences provided new empirical evidences of the continuity of structures of living systems even though various individuals of different types become incarnate or expressed these forms in kaleidoscopic patterns as the evolving system is shuffled. We shared the view that man's sense of self-esteem and worth in the long run required a perspective of meaning and value that transcended the uncertain life and accomplishments of his present bodily duration. We felt that the sciences were confirming the wisdom that ancient religions had perceived in answer to this need, although the scientific pictures were different in detail. My own thinking and writing about the continuity of life in what I call my doctrine of man's soul has been much stimulated by many conversations with Swami Akhilananda.

Zygon: Journal of Religion and Science
Chicago, Illinois

AMIYA CHAKRAVARTY

"A saint preaches sermons," wrote Thomas Merton, "by the way he walks and the way he stands—the way he picks things up and holds them in his hands." This is one way of saying that saintliness is not an extra quality, but a pervasive oneness that touches every aspect of a person's life until the most seemingly trivial things he does are a part of a unitive and wondrous purity.

When I think of Swami Akhilananda (and I knew him in Boston for over a decade), this oneness and simplicity, so characteristic of his radiant personality, shine in my memory. You looked at his face lighted up by an inner goodness, heard his strong, gentle voice, felt his deep concern for everyone who came into his life, listened to his sermons or his passing conversations, or met him in the kitchen where he excitedly (and dexterously) cooked meals for his many guests; you knew the essential rightness which was Akhilananda.

Yet this man of light knew sorrow. His "spiritual gaiety" was a daily conquest of suffering not only during the last few years when he was in physical pain; it was a conquest of evil and harm in a war-torn world where he shared the untold wrong inflicted on helpless, innocent multitudes. He drew people of every level and condition who brought their secret grief and torn, confused lives to this friendly priest and psychologist from faraway. He knew the anguish of racial victims, the plight of economically deprived and desperate individuals, the daily toll of broken homes. What he did for them was more than to provide compensatory religiosity or sooth-saying: he often changed their lives. His material gift to those in need was never merely a confidential and token assistance but a follow-through in terms of being admitted to a hospital, or finding a job, or helping to mend home life. Much more than this, it was always a prayerful act, a total gift of love. In much of this work he was helped by those who had local influence and contacts; but hardly anyone outside an intimate circle knew the details, and often the entire situation and the remedial steps were locked up in his sacred, lonely silence. Before he came to Boston he had already served during famines and in acutely distressed slum areas in India. He had been initiated as a swami of the Ramakrishna Order which practiced religion as a concrete, consecrated union of action and meditation. When he came to the West, the spirit of Christianity and prophetic Judaism reached him and supported his faith, as is also evidenced in his published books and courageous sermons.

Apart from his many contacts with religious leaders, both in the Boston area and in a widening circle all over this country, he was at home with workers in different aspects of medicine, especially psychiatry, though he had his reservations. He moved freely among humanists and intellectuals who had no institutional religious connections. He was also close to Unitarian ministers and movements whose religious affiliations were deep though unconventional. His prime quest was, in Dr. Radhakrishnan's words, for a "fellowship of the spirit" and this he gained among young students, business groups, and men and women in a variety of vocations and personal loyalties. Boston University, near which his Vedanta Center was located, provided him with rich fellowship at all levels: the School of Theology, then guided by Dean Walter G. Muelder, for whom we all felt profound devotion, inspired and strengthened him.

The Swami's theological position was not identical with institutional Christianity, but we all sensed a still deeper bond of human divinity which perhaps lies "beyond theology," that is to say, beyond all doctrinal and institutional boundaries. Through the Swami I met two great men, his friends in Cambridge, Professors Pitirim Sorokin and Gordon Allport. I shall never forget the joyous friendship which we shared. Sorokin's "altruism," perhaps one of the greatest contributions of our age, combined practical steps with an indomitable faith in humanity; at once original, intellectual, and far-reaching in its social applications, his guidance in theory and practice pointed toward a more neighborly and consciously active human race. Personally the great savant exemplified "altruistic love" in his radiant faith which stretched beyond all institutions; his ideas, practical and real, flowered in deep beauty wherever they were seeded with care, like the azaleas in his fabulous garden, to which Mrs. Sorokin and he often invited us. Gordon Allport laid a firm psychological and social basis for a humanity which belonged to all men and women, across the barriers of race, religion, and nation-stateism. Both these men accepted the Swami as a supreme spiritual leader.

What can I add in my tribute to a person whose saintliness was a gentle light and a challenging flame to many of us? Thomas Merton, a man of faith and vision, wrote the words which I have already used about the uniqueness and oneness of a spiritual personality. This quality was recognized by all who knew Swami Akhilananda, even by those who had met him once or knew him slightly. I remember the scene in the funeral parlor, where nurses, doctors, next-door shop-owners, and bell-boys from a nearby hotel gathered with his friends and colleagues to have a last glimpse of a serene personality whose acts and thoughts were united in dedicated love. Death could but confirm and never break that divinely human unity.

New York State University
New Paltz, New York

❧

WALTER HOUSTON CLARK

My first contact with Swami Akhilananda came at one of the early meetings of the Society for the Scientific Study of Religion at Harvard University about 1951 or 1952. From that time on until his death he attended practically all of the meetings of the Society and made important contributions to its programs. As one of the co-founders and officers of the new Society I much appreciated the positive support and encouragement the Swami gave. Our friendship grew warmer with each contact, and I always felt an empathy with him that he gave every evidence of reciprocating.

Several years after I first met him, both of us were asked by Professor Pitirim A. Sorokin, the distinguished founder of the Department of Sociology at Harvard, to become founding members of his Research Society for Creative Altruism, along with Igor Sikorsky, F. S. C. Northrop, Senator Ralph Flanders, Henry Margenau, A. H. Maslow, President Daniel Marsh of Boston University and other distinguished men. With his pregnant intuitive insights concerning the nature of society and his enormous energies Dr. Sorokin was a creative genius, though not strong in the patience and tact that such a collection of intellectuals required if the Society were to emerge as the viable and influential scholarly society that it deserved to be. Largely because of friction with the Administrative Director and some of the members of the Council, the Research Society foundered several years later after some achievements but with very little money raised. I can remember very vividly several of the stormy Council meetings that threatened the demise of the Society even earlier than it actually occurred. Those of us on the Council who were Christian required the calming and tolerant offices of the Hindu Swami to remind us that patience and a focus on our great goals were an essential if the Society were to achieve its purpose. This he did with patience and a wit that again and again served to pour oil on troubled waters.

A third society which we both supported was the Institute of Religion in an Age of Science. This had been founded in the early 1950's by Professor Ralph Wendell Burhoe, then Executive Officer of the American Academy of Arts and Sciences, with the idea of bringing together both religious scholars and scientists along with others interested in the problems of *rapprochement* between science and religion. The chief activity of the Institute continues to be the yearly program of lectures and discussions lasting a week each summer on the Isles of Shoals off the New Hampshire coast. Many distinguished scientists have lectured and participated in the activities of the

164

Institute. But for some reason it had always been difficult to secure the participation of as many religious scholars of equal eminence. This meant the dominance of the conferences by scientists and those who followed their leadership, with the result that the dialogue intended by the Institute became somewhat one-sided. There was a tendency for religion, as seen by the Institute, to become merely science dressed up in another suit of clothes.

But there was a small group of members, among whom were the Swami, Dr. James Houston Shrader, and I, who deplored this situation. All of us thoroughly supported the Institute and were committed to its emphasis on the need of a more thorough understanding of the nature of science by religious people, but we felt that a proper understanding of the importance of the nonrational, more "spiritual" and mystical component in religion was often left out. I can remember some of the intimate conversations between the three of us on the porch of the Hotel Oceanic on Star Island overlooking the harbor with stretches of the ocean beyond. And I can recall the Swami's amusement at the readiness with which many ultra-liberal people would uncritically accept benighted religious views provided only that the speaker wore the yellow robes of an Eastern ascetic rather than the sober apparel of a Southern Baptist preacher.

It was in this era of our friendship, about 1959 or 1960, when I was Dean of the Hartford School of Religious Education at the Hartford Seminary Foundation, that I brought the Swami to Hartford to give a lecture on the place of religion in psychotherapy. While I have now forgotten the details of that address, I can remember with much vividness and pleasure the effect of the Swami's warm personality and spiritual acumen on the students there. Some of them struck up a friendship with him that was still functioning at the time of his death. It gave me a glimpse into the sources of his influence with Christian youth, whose beliefs in the mystical values of Christianity were thereby strengthened.

In 1961 the Swami and I had dinner together when we met at a meeting in Chicago. He was limited in his diet and spoke of having to live carefully on account of some disorder. Also at the yearly dinner of the Massachusetts Vedanta Society on the Anniversary of Sri Ramakrishna in the spring of the same year the Swami was unable to prepare the food, as had been his custom. Since he was otherwise his old self and did not make much of his illness, I did not realize its seriousness. But when I first came to Andover-Newton Theological School as a visiting professor in the fall of 1961 and tried to get in touch with him I was told that he could not see anyone. However, I was finally allowed to visit him on his sickbed at the Boston Vedanta headquarters on Deerfield Street during that winter, when I said what proved to be the final good-bye to my old friend.

During the nineteenth and the first part of the twentieth centuries Christian missionaries trooped in large numbers to the East, mostly with the purpose of converting Eastern peoples to Christianity. Now the flow has begun to start in the opposite direction. The Swami was one of the early representatives of this reverse tide when when he came over from India in 1926 as a Hindu and member of the Ramakrishna Order with the purpose of interpreting Hinduism and Eastern religious thought to the United States. I never knew him to engage in proselytizing, and I never felt anything from him but a keen appreciation for my Christian convictions expressed in such a manner as to heighten my understanding of Jesus and to strengthen my sensitivities to the mystical and eternal values of Christianity. At the same time the quality of his life and personality could not but throw the most favorable light on his own Hinduism.

One of the Swami's most delightful characteristics was his sense of humor, which sometimes was useful to him in turning aside criticism. For example, there was once published a book written by a conservative Christian scholar who issued dark warnings of the dangers of many contemporaries subversive of what the writer considered the true faith. These consisted of almost all influential persons departing from mainline Protestant Christianity. I can remember the amusement of the Swami, shared by his friends, at his being considered one of these dangerous subversives. I never knew him to cast a slur on anyone's faith, and I never knew anyone who disliked him. As to his threat to Christianity, I several times told him that he was "the best Christian" I knew. This witticism always drew a chuckle from him, but underneath it pleased him, for in the essential sense he knew that I meant it.

In the broadest possible sense the contribution of Swami Akhilananda was the lessening of cultural gaps between the East and the West. With a grounding in Western science and culture through his studies in India and with an empathy for them and an interest in them, the Swami came to the United States to perform what became his life's mission. Hospitable to all walks of people, he was nevertheless most at home with intellectuals like himself, students, scholars, and scientists, particularly those who shared his devotion to the religious quest, even though few had advanced along the path as far as he. Professors Pitirim Sorokin, Gordon W. Allport, Robert Ulich, and O. Hobart Mowrer, as well as Clarence Faust and Dean Walter G. Muelder, were examples of the type of person he sought out as friends. To them he not only imparted his own wisdom but he also was open to learning from them in what was a truly creative dialogue. It was not in his nature to be authoritarian, narrow, or intolerant either in his teaching or his writing, and it was his humility that brought out the wisdom in others at the same time that it recommended his own.

His writings summed up his own particular part in the dialogue between East and West, to which he contributed so much understanding. For example, his *Hindu Psychology*, which appeared in 1946, was far ahead of its time, and I cannot but speculate that, had it made its first appearance today, it would have achieved a much wider circulation. That there are far more psychologists and general readers now open to its message is partly due to the patient spade work done a generation ago by the Swami and his collaborators. Youth, and particularly the members of the contemporary counter-culture, are much more interested in Oriental psychology and religion than was the case in the 1940's. *Hindu Psychology* differed from typical Western texts largely in the much greater space given to considerations of a religious and mystical nature. The taking seriously of paranormal phenomena, an emphasis on the "super-conscious," and discussion of the more positive aspects of the personality in the place of the Freudian concern with its more dismal sides were emphases that would now strike a very up-to-date chord.

Despite the Swami's winsomeness, charm, and appreciation of the religious traditions of the West, he was not without his disapprovals relative to such things as the mischievousness of a certain type of Christian missionary in the Orient which paved the way for imperialism whether of the political or commercial variety. He was sensitive to the harm done to Indian liberties in the days of its British overlords and more recent material exploitation from the West, and he did not hestitate to point out to missionaries who supported such things their departure from the teachings of their Master. At the same time he was big enough to appreciate the essential teachings of Christ, which he uttered never so eloquently as in his own devotion to Jesus and the incorporation of Christlike qualities into his own life.

But in his writings in the fields of both psychology and religion the most important message the Swami brought to us from the East was his emphasis on the mystical roots of religion, so much more fully developed in the East and so much needed in the overly rational and materialistic West. In part this was the legacy of Sri Ramakrishna, in part the teachings of his Order, in part the inspiration of his immediate guru Brahmananda, and in part the genius of the religious tradition of the East in which his development was embedded. In mysticism lie the roots of religion, neglected and largely forgotten even by those who stand to profit the most by it, the members of the Western religious institutions. It was in this area that Swami Akhilananda felt most keenly the impoverishment of the religion of the West. Doubtless he would agree with the words of one Western psychologist often quoted in his books, William James:

The mother sea and fountainhead of all religions lie in the

mystical experiences of the individual, taking the word mystical in a very wide sense. All theologies and all ecclesiasticisms
are secondary growths superimposed. . . .

This was the kernel of the message Swami Akhilananda brought
to the West.

Andover-Newton Theological School
Newton Centre, Massachusetts

❦

SRIMATA GAYATRI DEVI

Swami Akhilananda, a monk of the Ramakrishna Order of
India, first came to the United States in 1926 in order to assist
Swami Paramananda, another swami from the same Order.
Swami Paramananda had already established two centers, one in
Boston and another—a large ashrama or religious retreat—in
Southern California, for the purpose of teaching Vedanta.

On this sea voyage starting from Calcutta, I was Swami
Paramananda's other travelling companion. Being quite shy and
retiring, especially in relation to men, I did not even venture
to become acquainted with Swami Akhilananda, although both
of us came to this country to be resident members of each Center. However, I do remember how very gentle and soft-spoken
he was.

Several years later, after Swami Akhilananda had founded
an independent center in Providence, Rhode Island, he frequently invited Swami Paramananda to visit. I often went with
him together with other members of the community. I remember how Swami Akhilananda himself prepared the delicious
Hindu meals and served them to us. He was a very gracious
host and I can visualize his pleasing smile as we expressed appreciation for his hospitality. Only rarely did I have the opportunity to hear him speak. That is when he came to our center
during Swami Paramananda's lifetime on such occasions as the

public birthday celebration of Sri Ramakrishna or Swami Vivekananda.

Swami Akhilananda was always quiet, dignified and reserved. His distinction was in being a worthy spiritual descendant of Sri Ramakrishna, the Master Prophet of new India. For thirty-five years, Swami Akhilananda moved in academic and religious circles in the West, sharing the knowledge and wisdom which sprang from his religious devotion and dedicated life.

Ananda-Ashrama
La Crescenta, California

❦

L. HAROLD DeWOLF

My introduction to Swami Akhilananda came through the colleague who had been my major professor for doctoral studies in philosophy, Edgar S. Brightman. Dr. Brightman had an especially deep and personal appreciation and affection for the gifted leader of the Ramakrishna Society in Boston. If he were living on earth today he would be writing this note of personal reminiscence, for which he would be better qualified than I.

In a way theirs was a strangely antithetical relationship. Brightman was the rigorous logician par excellence. He was always deftly exposing the contradictions between the professions and practice of the government and of the church, while guiding his students to see and seek to eradicate the inconsistencies in their own thoughts and lives. To be sure, Brightman's was an organic logic, owing much to Hegel. He sought to find the larger truth beyond present conflict. However, that truth must itself be free of contradiction. The one teaching of his own mentor, Borden Parker Bowne, which he often castigated was Bowne's saying, "Life is greater than logic." Brightman acknowledged that life was *more* than logic, for it has content as well as form, color and pain as well as quantity and law. But Bowne had in his personalistic thought a streak of anti-rationalism which Brightman firmly rejected.

On the other hand, Akhilananda lived easily with contradictions, finding all of them transcended and reconciled "on the mystical level," beyond all formulas of rational statement.

Nevertheless, Brightman generously acknowledged that the Swami was a helpful spiritual guide, a guru to him. I am not quite sure what it was that Brightman most appreciatively learned from him. His indebtedness seemed to be for an opening of his mind to non-rational premises in prayer life and for psychological techniques or prayer disciplines to prepare his soul for mystical experience of God. Brightman remained an unequivocal Christian, his faith rooted in the Bible. But his belief that God reveals himself also in nature and especially in human nature in all times and places made him welcome the evidences of God's grace in Swami Akhilananda's kindly testimony and personality.

My personal memories of the Swami include many friendly discussions of philosophy and religion in his headquarters home on Bay State Road, a nearby restaurant, and my own home; a memorable meeting with Prime Minister Jawaharlal Nehru at the Ramakrishna Center; Akhilananda's speaking, at my request, in the chapel of Boston University College of Liberal Arts; and his invitation, which I accepted, to be the speaker at the Sunday service in the Center. In the college chapel he spoke on criteria by which one could judge whether a person who claimed to have experienced the presence of God had, in fact, or whether he might be deceiving or self-deceived. I do not remember many details, but I recall with appreciation his emphasis, like that of Jesus, on the idea that "by their fruits you shall know them." The closer a person's acquaintance with God, he said, the more his life would show a sensitive, loving concern for other people.

While Swami Akhilananda and I found wide areas of congenial thought, we found also occasion to debate vigorously some issues. He believed that Jesus was God and knew that he was, but that he was not actually a man and therefore could not have suffered or died in actuality. He only appeared to suffer and die in order to teach us how to accept pain and death. Consequently, although the Swami often assured Christian people that he believed in the incarnation, he did not in the historic Christian sense. What he called the incarnation of Christ was rather one of a number of appearances of God in what only appeared to be a human life. That is, Jesus was an *avatar*. Hence, when Akhilananda assured me, as he often did, that he accepted the Christian faith, as also other faiths, I contended that this claim was based on a misunderstanding.

His interpretation of the incarnation was one aspect of a wider difference between his Eastern mysticism and Christian world-views. Authentic Christians understand the material world to be a creation of God and believe that we have the privilege and responsibility so to use our bodies and all physical relationships as to make them instruments of God's loving purpose. Over against this incarnational and sacramental understanding of the body, the Swami espoused the view that the body and the whole material world constituted a lower realm of illusion above which we were called to rise by spiritual disciplines. The spiritual he thus set over against and above the material.

This difference came into especially sharp practical focus when a young American disciple of the Swami became engaged to marry a young Christian woman. After invitations for the wedding had been mailed, the young woman had some misgivings and came to me for counsel. Although the young man said he accepted all the Christian beliefs and much more besides, his fiancée still wondered whether there might be problems which could arise later if not confronted now. I suggested that for the sake of their future, she might well inquire of him what he would regard as the meaning of sexual union in marriage, in relation to his spiritual ideal. She turned to tell me in dismay that he considered the ideal marriage to be one in which the husband and wife lived in spiritual companionship but never touched each other. The issue came to a climax when the two came to my office together to explore further. The young man assured his intended bride that he was no saint and she need not fear that he would become a celibate husband. But bursting into tears she declared that she did not want to be a temptation, keeping him from his ideal. She wanted a husband who would see the marital relationships with her as belonging to the sacred heights of life, not as a sign and force of his spiritual failure. The two were counseling with the Swami also and he tried to reassure the young woman that she had no cause for worry. Yet the more they talked the more the issue seemed clear to her and in great sorrow she finally broke the engagement. Here in practical terms was demonstrated the great divide between Oriental mysticism, however generously eclectic, on the one side, and the Judeo-Christian attitude toward life, on the other.

The one other issue on which Swami Akhilananda and I most sharply differed—though always in warm personal friendship—came to the surface at the time his book *Hindu Psychology* was being published. We met for lunch and a long talk together, in a hotel restaurant near the Center. That day we talked about metaphysical monism and the views which he called dualistic and which Western theistic philosophers called pluralistic. The question was whether a human person is an aspect or moment of God himself—as the monist believes—or whether a man and God are two, so that there are many personal beings including both God and all the persons he has created. In that conversation we were in hearty agreement as we shared the arguments against monism and in favor of the view that God is other than any human person. In fact the Swami laughed gaily—and he always laughed easily—as we talked about the irrational contradictions involved in monism. As a man makes mistakes or sins, is God making the mistakes but at the same time knowing the truth, both as other men know the truth and as God in his eternal perfection knows it? What nonsense! Does God sin in our sin, but at the same time live in sinless perfection? We agreed that such absurd and blasphemous conclusions follow with inevitable logic from the monistic

173

view and so we laughed at its absurdity. I was a little surprised at our agreement but it could not have seemed clearer or more unequivocal.

At the same meeting the Swami gave me a copy of his new book and asked that after I had read it I meet him again and talk about it. I started reading that night and finished within the next two days. So it was that we met again for lunch, in the same place, exactly one week after our first discussion of monism. I reported that while I had found the book beautifully written and often insightful, I had been perplexed to find it apparently defending the very monism which he and I had joined in rejecting a week ago. Had I misunderstood? The Swami laughed and laughed. Then he said he could easily understand my feeling. "You see," he said, "when we were talking before, we were considering the question on the logical level. On that level monism is absurd. But the book moves to the mystical level and there monism is true."

Such radical and basic changes of view according to context seemed to me a quite intolerable equivocation bordering on intellectual dishonesty, though I did not doubt that the Swami's own moral intention was upright. Our discussion led him to say, I thought with substantial exaggeration, that he agreed with me on everything excepting my "intolerance"!

Here, then, are some basic issues. Vedantism has little concern with trying to change the world with its racism and injustice, though winsomely teaching personal lovingkindness, beautifully exemplified by Swami Akhilananda. For all things have their place on some level. Besides, our vocation is not to change the material, earthly order of things but to rise above it into pure spirituality.

In any event, I believe that Christians ought not to raise barriers against open discussion with people of other faiths. We ought to learn all we can from them—and there is much of good to be learned—while sharing our own faith and thanking God for the evidence that he has not restricted his revealing love to one stream of history but has sought all human beings in all times and places. The reader must make up his own mind on the issues posed by Swami Akhilananda's able writing. In this writing will be encountered eclectic Hinduism at its best, a Hinduism deeply influenced by Christian teaching. Let the reader not be beguiled into supposing that there are no issues here. They are profound and far-reaching. So much the greater is the reason for reading both with open mind and with critical alertness the work of this humane, thoughtful, and saintly Vedantist.

Wesley Theological Seminary
Washington, District of Columbia

❦

DANA L. FARNSWORTH

My friendship with Swami Akhilananda began while I was Director of the Medical Department of the Massachusetts Institute of Technology from 1946 to 1954 during one year of which I was Acting Dean of Students. It continued after I became Director of the University Health Services at Harvard in 1954 and continued until his untimely death in 1962.

Our association came about because both of us had students in distress from time to time who came to us for counseling.

What stands out most prominently in my mind was his patience and tolerance with the weaknesses and foibles of the people he tried to help. He could see through pretense and insincerity without becoming moralistic and judgmental because he respected every person even though he could not approve all his behavior.

His sense of humor carried him through many a trying situation. It was also an added element in the attractiveness of his personality, especially when I was a guest in his home or he in mine.

His emphasis on the good points of all religions rather than a critical attitude toward others than those most favored was heart-warming. In times like these, when suspicion of all groups, religious or otherwise, is almost universal, persons of his quality are sorely needed.

His colleagues in his many community activities were a varied group, all characterized by a profound concern for the human situation but working toward its betterment in a wide variety of ways.

He came as near to representing and practicing the gentle ethic of Christianity as any Christian could. The greatest tribute we can pay to his memory is to apply the spiritual principles he supported in word and deed to all our activities. In his words, "then alone can humanity find peace."

Harvard University
Cambridge, Massachusetts

❦

CLARENCE H. FAUST

Swami Akhilananda and I were good friends for a long time in spite of philosophical and religious differences and almost diametrically opposed views of the methods for acquiring, nurturing, and making commitment to truth in these areas.

We met in the early fifties as members of an interesting group which had been brought together by the Chancellor of the Jewish Theological Seminary of America, Rabbi Louis Finkelstein, and which called itself The Conference on Science, Philosophy, and Religion. The group consisted of people of strong and often sharply divergent views on questions of the day. It was an interdisciplinary and interfaith group. It included Catholic leaders, such as Father John LaFarge, S.J., and Father John Courtney Murray; Protestants, such as F. Ernest Johnson of Teachers' College, Columbia, and Dean Liston Pope of Yale

Divinity School; Jewish leaders, such as Louis Finkelstein himself and his Vice-Chancellor, Simon Greenberg. There were scientists, such as Nobel Prize winner I. I. Rabi of Columbia University, Hudson Hoagland, Director of the Worcester Foundation for Experimental Biology, and Harvard's distinguished astronomer Harlow Shapley. There were, too, scholars, such as the University of Chicago philosopher Richard R. McKeon, the Columbia University sociologist R. M. MacIver, and Yale's Harold Lasswell.

The group met several times a year for a weekend of discussion at an attractive old Quaker inn called Mohonk near Poughkeepsie, New York.

The agenda likely consisted of whatever happened to be on the participants' minds. The discussions were serious and sometimes heated. On occasion the dialogue was brilliant. Sometimes agreement was reached to pursue in greater depth a topic all agreed to be important, and a conference would be planned at which experts or "resource persons," as they are now commonly called, would be invited, along with regular members of the group, to prepare and read papers. The conference proceedings were then published as a book. There were about twenty such books over the years, including *Freedom and Authority in Our Time*, *Aspects of Human Equality*, *The Ethics of Power: the Interplay of Religion, Philosophy and Politics*, and *Approaches to Education for Character*.

Swami Akhilananda was brought into the group, as I recall it, by one of the scientists who knew of his work as a student counselor at Massachusetts Institute of Technology. To impress or win the respect of such a group was not easy, especially for someone holding the Swami's views, which we Westerners tend to regard, at least to begin with, as unworthy of serious consideration.

But the Swami soon did win the respect of the group. At the outset he seemed rather shy in what must often have struck him as a hurly-burly of strong-minded, rather aggressively talkative people. He limited himself almost wholly to infrequent questions and suggestions put forward somewhat hesitantly. But most of us soon noticed that his questions and suggestions were very much worth attention. He spoke somewhat hesitantly as if anxious to avoid any appearance of animus toward an individual or any impression of taking the first step in an assault on a position he intended to demolish. His questions were never rhetorical questions as too many of those raised by others were, but expressed a real desire to know and to learn. His suggestions tended to be proposals for bridges across chasms that appeared to separate sharply opposed, even contradictory, views and opinions.

In all this he reflected a rare kind of tolerance: not the tolerance of indifference in which one politely and patiently suffers another's ideas or system of ideas because they seem to have no bearing on what one regards as really important; but rather the kind of tolerance of a man of strongly-founded, well-considered views who yet respects someone holding opposed, or seemingly opposed, views enough to want to understand the other in the hope of finding, if possible, the ground of mutual modification that would while getting rid of conflict enrich both positions. This mode of discussion was sufficiently rare and so clearly valuable as practiced by the Swami that his respect for others won in turn the respect of a large majority of the group.

The Swami and I had many meetings apart from those of the conference, mostly when his work brought him to New York. In these, he and I faced in the manner just sketched our own apparently irreconcilable differences about the proper method of acquiring and developing religious and philosophical knowledge. I was at the time a self-confident rationalist of the eighteenth century kind, my field of study and teaching being eighteenth century literature. For those who like labels, I might have been tagged a belated Deist and my religious beliefs even now tagged as Neo-Deism. I thought of the Swami at first as an interesting, and, as time went on, a lovable and highly intelligent representative of Oriental mysticism.

When I contrasted what I thought of as painstaking and sound rationalism with the apparently easy and sudden illumination of mysticism, disparaging the latter, the Swami would in response talk about the religious exercises which he said prepared a person through a difficult discipline for what I called sudden mystical experience and insights. I therefore began to try to find out just what these "exercises" or "practices" were and how they functioned. I learned a good deal, although not all I wanted to know.

It was in these conversations that I urged the Swami, as he is kind enough to remember in his book *Spiritual Practices*, to publish his views and experiences in such exercises. When I saw the manuscript he wrote, I was pleasantly surprised by the reference in it to my stimulating him to do the book.

It is a pleasure to welcome this new edition of the work. Many readers, I think, will find in it the lovable and admirable character of Swami Akhilananda and, perhaps especially in the chapter "What is Mysticism?," the stimulus to thoughtfulness and meditation he provided in life to his many friends.

Claremont, California

❦

DANA McLEAN GREELEY

One of the most gentle and persuasive religious leaders of the last generation in Boston and in America was Swami Akhilananda, whose affectionate spirit and generous life exemplified religion at its very best. His modesty was as great as his competence, and he was at home among the intellectuals and the literati, on the one hand, and the meek and the poor in spirit, on the other hand. I knew him at conferences on religion and science at the Isles of Shoals in New Hampshire, where the religionists and the scientists equally respected him, at inter-faith discursive and celebrative occasions alike, at the great Cathedral of the Pines out under the open sky in New Hampshire, and at the intimate gatherings at the Vedanta Center on Deerfield Street in Boston. He was always the same person, reflecting the divine spirit that was within him and intensely interested in and considerate of other people.

He was as business-like, I am sure, in practical affairs as he was spiritual in religion and philosophical with the scholars. And he loved America as much as he loved his never-to-be-forgotten India. He had a profound faith of his own but he was also completely tolerant and appreciative of other faiths; and he was as adept at dialogue as he was profound in both personal and communal mysticism. My wife and I shall always carry with us the inspiration of both his hospitality and his friendship.

First Parish in Concord
Concord, Massachusetts

❦

PAUL E. JOHNSON

I first met Swami Akhilananda some thirty years ago when we were co-speakers in a lecture series arranged by the Community Church of Boston. Immediately I was impressed by his radiant, loving spirit, and his profound depth of religious experience and understanding.

From that time we were frequently in touch with each other. My wife and I were often invited to his Vedanta Center on Bay State Road in Boston, where he generously served us delicious food prepared with his own loving hands. He recalled that when he first joined the Vedanta order it was his responsibility to provide the meals for the brothers who gathered together around Swami Brahmananda. When he came to our home he took a special interest in our children and they will never forget him.

He graciously invited me to attend his personal worship at the Ramakrishna Chapel, Deerfield Street, Boston, on Decem-

180

ber 18, 1943. This I described, with his permission, in the first edition of my *Psychology of Religion* (Nashville: Abingdon Press, 1945), pages 138-139. The altar of carved mahogany was dedicated to God with the Sanskrit character *Om*, and the motto: "Truth is One, men call it by various names."

The Swami entered, removed his shoes, and seated himself before the altar, legs crossed, hands folded, eyes closed in prayer. Then he devoted himself to the earnest drama of the human spirit communing with the Spirit of God for two hours in the following order:

1. Consecration of the room.

2. Invocation, asking the blessings of the different aspects of God.

3. He prayed:

"May thou be installed in the hearts of all devotees. May thou be the source of their knowledge. May the divine love be with them. We are worshipping thee that thy eternal glory may be with all, that all beings may be illumined and led to thy realization."

4. Removal of evil influences from the room with flowers, rice, and mustard seed; drawing a line of light around the worshiper and devotees, clapping and snapping fingers around his head.

5. Consecration of water for worship with gestures, prayers, and blessings.

6. Purification of the prayer rug with prayers and flowers.

7. Purification of flowers and other emblems of worship, including large trays of various fruits, milk, honey, and holy water from the Ganges River.

8. Transformation of the body by awakening latent divine power through gestures and prayers.

9. *Pranayama*, or rhythmic breathing through alternate nostrils.

10. Awakening the mystic centers of the body by praying, chanting, and touching these areas of the body.

11. Worship of the different aspects of God—creative and sustaining; and the different powers and incarnations, includ-

ing Christ, Buddha, Krishna and others, with offerings of perfume, flowers, incense, light, and food.

12. *Dhyana*, or meditation in silence—body poised, eyes closed, and mind focused in concentration.

13. Consecration of the various aspects of the body, mind, and emotions of love, patience, devotion, etc.

14. Worship of the particular aspect of God for the day, with offerings of flowers, milk, honey, water, use of a bell, relics, mystic circles with incense, kneeling, and chanting.

15. Reading from the Gospel of John, chapter 1.

16. Surrender of the fruit of worship to God.

17. Benediction: a prayer for peace, harmony, joy, and bliss in the world.

Later in the conversation with me he gave me a personal name on which to focus my worship. This name was "Christ".

In his book *Hindu View of Christ* he affirms how deeply he believed the incarnation of the one God in Christ. He also shows how God incarnates himself in other great religious leaders.

The witness of this is clearly given in the Old Testament heroes of the faith, as well as the disciples and apostles of the New Testament. This became the central affirmation of the disciples, and Jesus said to them, "As the Father hath sent me, so send I you" (John 20:21). Paul declared, "For me to live is Christ" (Philippians 1:21).

Swami Akhilananda was a devout Hindu. Yet he was one of the best Christians I have known. Not only did he believe in the incarnation of God in Christ, but he faithfully followed his teachings and way of life as a guiding light and inexhaustible source of power. Association with him awakened and strengthened my faith in Christ as the incarnation of God, and the hope that God may be incarnate in each of us.

Centerville, Massachusetts

JOHN H. LAVELY

Even though Swami Akhilananda died in 1962 and Dr. Edgar S. Brightman died in 1953, I can still see them as clearly as though it were yesterday: engaged in animated conversation, deeply serious yet strangely light-hearted, pressing a point and yielding a point, never in perfect agreement but always learning from each other. One could only envy a friendship which produced such conversation. What a model for the relation of East and West, this friendship between the American philosopher and the seer from India.

I cannot think of one of these friends without thinking of the other. Indeed, it was through Dr. Brightman, my beloved teacher and later colleague at Boston University, that I became acquainted with the Swami. And it is to a few recollections of the Swami that I want to confine myself here.

The image under which I like to think of Swami Akhilananda is that of a missionary in a foreign land. I hasten to add that I do not mean by missionary a proselytizer, which the Swami most emphatically was not. Although he established and presided over the Ramakrishna Vedanta Center in Boston (and one in Providence) for many years, he was not primarily interested in getting formal adherents or in advocating a doctrinal truth. Nevertheless, he had a spiritual mission, to which he was totally committed. He aimed completely to assist people to realize the goal of life—direct experience of ultimate Reality or God—by a variety of spiritual disciplines and practices. He did not feel that this goal was the exclusive custody of any particular tradition. He was, therefore, hospitable to the religious dimension of all the great faiths.

Because of this kind of devotional ecumenicism, he was able to appeal to a surprisingly wide spectrum of intellectuals in the Boston area. I think the thing that impressed me most about the Swami was the number of great minds he knew, in a personal way. For many of these he performed a pastoral function which no local clergyman could have. Of course, he was able to hold his own in sophisticated philosophical discussions (he was, for example, an active member of Philosophics Anonymous, an informal group of Boston area philosophers and theologians) but perhaps more important was his gift of providing practical guidance in spiritual matters. His was indeed a great ministry over the years in Boston.

Let me close this tribute to a unique spiritual leader with two specific recollections. The first has to do with the birthday parties for Sri Ramakrishna (and on one occasion the Mother). These were remarkable occasions, these annual celebrations to which the Swami invited his friends and for which he personally cooked and served superb Indian dishes. My impression is that upwards of two hundred people usually attended these festal occasions. And those of us who did will not soon forget these unusual events and the Swami who presided over them so graciously.

The second special recollection has to do with his emphasis on the reality and accessibility of "the superconscious experience" of God or ultimate Reality. The Swami was not only a practitioner of mysticism but also a philosophic interpreter of the mystical life in all traditions. I vividly recall his response to the challenge: How can you validate the ineffable and private mystic experience? I had expected the response I had so often heard before, namely, that the mystic experience validates itself. Not so the Swami. He made a point of saying that the test of the authenticity of the experience was the effect on and in the total life of the mystic. In other words, "By their fruits shall you know them." Or as the Swami puts it in *Spiritual Practices*: "The difference between hallucinations and mystical experience is this: The personality does not change for the better when an individual experiences hallucinations through use of drugs or in mental illness," but the personality does change for the better as a result of mystical experience. And judging by the quality of the Swami's saintly life, I would say that he knew whereof he spoke.

Boston University
Boston, Massachusetts

RICHARD M. MILLARD

The two words that come closest to describing Swami Akhilananda for me are "catholic" and "compassionate." His was a compassionate Catholicism that embraced all persons, things, and points of view. His religion embraced all religions synthesized in his own. His philosophy embraced all philosophies corrected through their mutual complementation. His humanity embraced all human beings in a universal love that accepted all of us as we are but corrected and compensated for our shortcomings, our weaknesses in the total family of humanity. For the Swami no one was ever really wicked or wrong, but incomplete; and he would have passed the same judgement upon himself and his sense of need for completion. As an individual he understood, forgave, admired, and loved.

As might be expected, this sense of love and admiration extended to the animal world as well as to the human beings. I remember one beautiful late-June evening on our porch in a suburb of Boston; the darkness had settled in, redolent of the moisture, warmth, and blossoms of early summer. The conversation somehow got around to the prescient dog in Van Paassen's *Days of Our Years*. The Swami suggested that not only is such prescience not uncommon—he had known many such instances—but that animals have far more intelligence, emotional involvement, and even understanding than most human beings give them credit for. He went on to suggest, not that other animals are superior to men, but that they may have more compassion for men than many men do for animals. For the animals, at least the higher ones, have a feeling for the whole and their place in it which human beings sometimes, through overzealousness and restricted vision, do not have. The animals not only suffer but suffer for people; while we in our short-sightedness, disrupt the natural harmony of which we are a part and to which we should recognize ourselves as belonging.

Since that time ecology has become a fashion, even a fad, but I have the feeling that the Swami had a sense of the belongingness of all things that makes much of our current ecological concern more surface than substance.

Education Commission of the States
Denver, Colorado

❦

CAROLE MOREAU

There are so few truly gifted people who can shed that special light on individuals whose lives have been darkened through various circumstances. Only those who personally knew Swami Akhilananda could feel and possibly explain that "special light." Through his light came hope, direction, abeyance of fears, as well as religious guidance. I mention religion lastly because he was not trying to convert. He was trying to help people find God in their way, not his way. He would tailor his knowledge and advice to fit their needs.

He was on call to humanity twenty-four hours a day. There were always numerous telephone conversations with disturbed persons. There would be an emergency call from a near-suicidal alcoholic whose life had atrophied to the size of a liquor bottle. But she did call for help and Swami would instantly go. No matter what a person's plight, Swami would indicate it was not a *great* misfortune. I suppose he was trying to say he believed there was no truly great tragedy in a person's life. Why, then, did he continuously offer advice, consolation, a hope for a better tomorrow? He gave form to people's lives. He made them active and resourceful. If he knew of any true tragedy a person could know, that was his secret. Of course, one can be made to see through one's own blindness of misery and acquire a taste for tomorrow. This, I believe, was his philosophy: giving hope, giving a line to life, and this man was always giving, always selfless.

He had a passion for peace. I once asked him what he wanted most in this world. He replied, "I would like world peace." Yet, in spite of his associations with many well-known people in various fields, he was and remained a modest person. He delivered no sense of superiority— even as he had seen Christ! It was arranged that his own picture be placed on the mantle in the library of the Boston Center. I recall him voicing discomfort over this gesture.

There were joyous times for him, too. He derived great pleasure preparing large dinners he would have occasionally at the Centers. I would watch him work, whistling, singing, and doing a little dance while the kettles boiled! He was happiest when he was busy, which was most of the time. His luncheons, lectures, and trips would take their toll, though, and he would become ill and need rest. Even then there would be activity: writing and dictating letters, making and receiving phone calls when he could.

He was a most tolerant man. The only thing that would irritate him was when he was rendered passive by illness. He was always happy to listen, to help. He wanted people to learn peace and to get along with each other.

He is a man who is deeply missed by all who knew and loved him. His teachings remain in our minds. His blessings remain in our hearts. What did he leave behind with us? No matter what our faults, we are always under the wing of God, should we just realize God is there. Life can fall into place if we learn to be at peace with ourselves and ask for guidance in helping others.[1]

Barrington, Rhode Island

---

[1] Carole Moreau is the granddaughter of Mrs. Anna M. Worcester, who was closely associated with the Swami's work for thirty-five years. For part of this time Mrs. Worcester had been asked to live at The Vedanta Center. Thus, her daughter and granddaughter also became members of the Swami's household. Mrs. Moreau spent the first twelve years of her life under the Swami's loving influence.

WALTER G. MUELDER

Not long after I assumed my duties at Boston University as Dean of the School of Theology in 1945 I became acquainted with Swami Akhilananda. He was already a friend of colleagues such as Edgar S. Brightman and Paul E. Johnson. Over the course of the years others like Jannette Newhall, L. Harold DeWolf, and Edwin P. Booth had frequent associations with him. In this way there was a most friendly attitude toward him and his work in the School. Various ones from time to time invited him to lecture in their classes, attended services at the Ramakrishna Vedanta Center, visited with him at lunch, or participated in the annual dinner celebrating the birthday of Sri Ramakrishna. Swami seemed to feel quite at home in the fellowship of our seminary faculty, partly because of these personal contacts, and partly, perhaps, because of a pervasive pacifist orientation among many faculty and students following World War II, their interests in Indian independence and in world religions, and their concern for spiritual growth and affirmation.

His coterie of Boston University friends in the fields of philosophy and religion was only part of a wider circle in greater Boston who admired and respected him. I was always quite aware of his concern for and ministry to colleagues at Massachusetts Institute of Technology, Harvard, and other educational centers in the metropolitan area. For all of these he was a kind of spiritual catalyst. One became aware of his wide circle of ministry to intellectual Bostonians when one attended the annual dinner. The diversity of disciplines represented was impressive, ranging from astronomy to sociology, psychology, and the humanities and from personnel administration to faculty spouses. The persons present might never see each other in the same cross-sections of interests on any other occasion. Their presence disclosed a mutuality of spiritual concern and breadth of religious openness which was meaningful to all. Such persons included Harlow Shapley, astronomer; Pitirim A. Sorokin, sociologist; Gordon Allport, psychologist; as well as those from Boston University mentioned above. The names of these persons appear in the prefaces to Swami's books and testify to the close intellectual and personal companionship he sustained with outstanding minds in Boston's leading universities. He was thoroughly versed in the writings of Sorokin, Allport, Johnson, and Brightman and with the viewpoints which conflicted with theirs.

At the dinners and often at the lunches at the Center Swami himself prepared much of the food. Such preparation was an act of devotion on his part directed to his own immediate spiritual master, to Sri Ramakrishna, and to the All-Loving One. He spoke often of his spiritual master, Swami Brahmananda, to whom all his books are dedicated. I often talked with him about his relationship with his beloved master and about his care in the preparation of food for special occasions.

My relationship with Swami was many-sided. Quite regularly we had lunch together either at the Center or in some pleasant restaurant like the Window Shop in Cambridge. We discussed the major ideas he was wrestling with in the American cultural scene, the secular challenges to religion, psychologies that seemed insensitive to the realities of spiritual experience, particularly troublesome issues in counseling, the needs of theological students, and the writing we were doing at the time.

Occasionally Swami discussed the experience of having clients who had had disappointing experiences with psychiatrists. He was very critical of professional persons who were technically well-trained but who did not really love people or who could not perceive the need for couples to love at the spiritual level. He had, of course, great trust and faith in the power of mature religious experience. He saw all of his pastoral ministry in the context of that being whom he called the All-loving One.

We enjoyed Swami's visits to our home. He always expressed keen interest in the children and their problems and development. He was sensitive toward the anxieties of mothers who carried heavy responsibilities of child-rearing as the wives of professionally ambitious and success-oriented men. He was pastoral counselor for youths and young adults from a number of such homes and for those from broken homes.

Professional men also came to see him. Professors of religion and ministers of the gospel were among those who cherished his friendship, his wisdom, and his guidance in spiritual practices. He took the initiative also in calling on them when ill and he remembered their family festivals. We often discussed the kinds of spiritual disciplines which he felt were appropriate for busy people in the American culture. In such matters his caring included respect for their religious traditions. He was well-read in the writings of Christian mysticism. With his guidance I read, as time permitted, in the literature of Vedanta and we discussed its methods in relation to Christian devotional living.

Swami and I had a limited colleague relationship in matters of worship. Once when he went to India for six weeks I took over the Sunday service at the Center on Deerfield Street in Boston. I could not, of course, lead the Vedanta worship service in the same way that he led it, but there was no problem basically, since he had so deep a reverence for Christ. At no time did I feel compromised in my personal commitments by participating as leader or visitor at the Center. For three of his books he requested that I write an introduction.

In our ultimate interpretation of religious faith and experience there were important philosophical differences, but he viewed these as different aspects or levels of spiritual realization. He was finally a monist and adhered to a non-dualistic view of God; i.e., a relationship of ultimate non-dualism between man and God. My personalistic metaphysics, which always distinguished man the worshipper and God the object of worship, held to communion rather than union. For Swami this dualistic level was authentic and true but not the highest stage of mystical experience. His model was the experience of his beloved Master and that of Ramakrishna; mine was Christian and strongly voluntaristic and communitarian. Sometimes we practiced meditation together. Those occasions were very meaningful and cemented our friendship with mutual trust.

Though I had a continuing interest in worship, prayer, and

mysticism, my teaching and writing were primarily in ethics and ecumenics. Swami always encouraged me in these matters, taking special interest in those issues involving methods of social change and assumptions regarding human nature and its development. He was distressed by the vast amount of violence in the world and the apparent ease with which many theologians accommodated to force and coercion for an alleged good end. He was particularly critical of theologians like Reinhold Niebuhr who seemed to rationalize war and who seemed too pessimistic about human nature. Swami held to non-violent action and supported the practical philosophy of Gandhi. Because of my participation in ecumenism he was very supportive in efforts that looked toward religious reconciliation. In his later years he frequently expressed the faith that soon some great break-through in the religious development of mankind would take place. He never specified what it would be.

In the face of physical suffering he was a patient and courageous man. He experienced a great deal of pain in his later years. He tried not to let it interfere with his ministry in Boston and Providence. Swami Akhilananda was a truly spiritual person and the power that was released within him radiated blessing among those with whom he practiced his mission.

Boston University School of Theology
Boston, Massachusetts

❦

JANNETTE E. NEWHALL

Swami Akhilananda was a warm and gentle spirit who commanded both respect and affection from those who knew him. My personal contacts with him were chiefly through the monthly meetings of a small group of professors from Andover-Newton Theological Seminary, Boston University, Episcopal

191

Theological School, Harvard, Tufts, and Wellesley, called "Philosophics Anonymous." Swami was a faithful attendant and took his turn at leading the discussions. His comments were always integrative rather than divisive. He had a great capacity to enter into the thought of another person and to feel kinship and sympathy. His kindly concern during the serious illness of my mother meant a great deal to me.

Boston University School of Theology
Boston, Massachusetts

❦

F. S. C. NORTHROP

Swami Akhilananda joyfully embodied in our midst "the psychic Atman which is the cosmic Brahman without differences" of his Vedantic Hindu religious roots and practices. At Providence, Boston, or New Haven, as well as Benares or Calcutta, he was its incarnation of the Divine. One's own personal friend, yet so spontaneous, open, outgoing, and cosmopolitan as to be *ipso facto* the equally special friend of all. Unqualifiedly of Ramakrishna's non-dualistic Vedantic North India, he was equally relaxed, informed, and at home in the America to which he gave the greater portion of his life. Affirming that "no religion has a monopoly on God," he entered into our Judaic-Christianity from within as well as collaboratively seeing the best in it from without, while helping us, at our lured initiative, to understand psychologically and experience practically his own religious psychology and its ways. Thereby he enriched both approaches to and components of the Divine for cosmic nature as well as his fellow men. Thus in warming our hearts he refreshed and enlarged our minds. It was an immanent, infinitely blissful feelingfulness which our Swami Akhilananda incarnated in our midst.

Judaism, Christianity, and Islam supplement rather than merely re-echo the thesis of Buddhism and our beloved Swami Akhilananda's unqualified nondualistic Vedantic Hinduism. This, he, with his heartwarming, joyful smile, would welcome and perhaps also want to qualify.

Yale University
New Haven, Connecticut

❦

SWAMI PRABHAVANANDA

It is very difficult for me to remember the events or the intimate talks that Swami Akhilananda and I may have had during our stay in Madras. We used to go out for walks along the beach. All I can say is that we loved each other very much.

It comes to my mind that Maharaj wanted to worship Mother Durga in the image in Madras the year Swami Akhilananda and I were there. The image was brought from Calcutta, and before Swami Akhilananda got his vows of *sannyas*, he performed the worship with the assistance of Swami Sharvananda, the abbot of the monastery. After that both Swami Akhilananda and I received *sannyas* together. That is why I used to call him my twin brother.

Several years later I was the first one sent to this country. During the time that I was head of the Portland center, Swami Prakashananda, head of the San Francisco center, asked me to come and receive Swami Akhilananda, Swami Paramananda, and Gayatri Devi. Swami Dayananda, who also came, remained as an assistant to Swami Prakashananda; and Swami Akhilananda became the assistant to Swami Paramananda in Boston. Swami Akhilananda later opened centers in Providence and Boston.

After giving charge of the Portland center to another Swami, I came to Los Angeles. Gradually a center was established with a convent in Santa Barbara, a monastery in Trabuco Canyon, and both a monastery and convent in Los Angeles. When the first vows of *Brahmacharya* were given to the nuns at the Sarada Convent in Santa Barbara, Swami Akhilananda and Mrs. Worcester came at my invitation. I also remember how he came one time to the Trabuco Monastery for the Fourth of July celebration. He gave a wonderful sermon which everyone appreciated. He came quite a few times to visit me, but I cannot remember the dates.

One year during the Durga Puja season he invited me to his center and paid my fare (this may have been the occasion of the dedication of the Providence center). A girl was present who was to be initiated by Swami Akhilananda. However, after hearing just one of my lectures, this girl requested initiation from me. Swami Akhilananda graciously asked me to initiate her, but of course, it could not be done.

I spoke to the girl and, when she insisted, said, "All right, you accept me as your guru; and as your guru, I am asking you to be initiated by Swami Akhilananda!"

Swami Akhilananda was a loving soul—having wonderful love for everyone. I was envious of his love for Maharaj, his guru. I remember one occasion when he visited here. We got together with other monastic members and asked him to speak about Maharaj. While he spoke he was sobbing and weeping. His love was so great.

Vedanta Society of Southern California
Hollywood, California

S. PAUL SCHILLING

The publication of this memorial edition of Swami Akhilananda's *Spiritual Practices* is a timely event, because he has something of critical importance to say to a world committed to—yet frequently disillusioned by—the allegedly practical values of scientific technology. Central in his teaching is a conviction shared by all great religions: that reality is deeper and richer than the phenomena accessible to sense perception, hence that our methods of knowing need to be broad enough to deal adequately with the whole range of data to be explored.

When I read the Swami I am reminded of the American poet Wallace Stevens, who insisted that a narrow realism corrupts the fullness of reality, and that there is actually no such thing as "a bare fact." In "times of inherent excellence," writes Stevens, we become aware of "a tidal undulation underneath" the surface appearances of our lives. At such times we are awakened to realities beyond ourselves, a world unfathomed by those who search prosaically for supposedly objective facts, a many-sided realm of dynamic, rhapsodic movement. Though the similarity between the two writers is obvious, the differences are also noteworthy. Whereas Stevens is content to hint at the divine character of the transcendent, Akhilananda identifies it emphatically as God, the ultimate Reality, the soul of the universe. Further, the Swami believes that the experience of God comes not only through unexpected encounters, but through the practice of spiritual disciplines which prepare the human spirit for communion with the divine.

Pragmatic Westerners sometimes charge Eastern mystics with other-worldliness and social irresponsibility. However valid this criticism may be in other instances, it cannot fairly be lodged against Akhilananda. In his view the person who is aware of God realizes that "the whole world is a veritable manifestation of God." This means that the believer cannot be indifferent to social problems. On the contrary, he must recognize that people whose basic physical needs are unmet cannot effectively cultivate the spiritual life or attain a mature consciousness of the divine presence. Food is "the problem of problems all over the world." Religious people must therefore be actively concerned about hunger, as well as the closely related questions of disease, poverty, and war.

The convictions mentioned here were for Swami Akhilananda not matters of theory alone; they were incarnated in his life and in all his relations with other people. In *Mahatma Gandhi: An Interpretation* Stanley Jones writes of Gandhi: "One of the most Christlike men in history was not called a Christian at all." These words might be appropriately applied to the Swami also. I remember well his gentleness of spirit and his sensitive regard for his fellow human beings. The quality of his life won a hearing for his message, for unquestionably something of God was manifested in him.

He deserves to be taken seriously in our time. Our day-by-day experience is full of intimations of transcendence. To rule them out as irrelevant to the quest for dependable knowledge of the world because they do not fit a preconceived norm of scientific objectivity would involve an indefensible impoverishment of our existence. To rule them in could lead us into the living presence of God himself. This is what happened in the life of Swami Akhilananda. Through years of serious devotion and joyful service he reached a consciousness of God which became the central fact of his experience. From this center flowed light and power that blessed all who knew him.

Wesley Theological Seminary
Washington, District of Columbia

JAMES HOUSTON SHRADER

I first met the Swami at a meeting of the Committee (later the Society) on the Scientific Study of Religion which met on the top floor of Emerson at Harvard. The Swami, in a smiling, gracious manner, rose to deny the allegations of a speaker who had declared that human experience was not valid evidence. After the meeting I sought him out and inquired further concerning his idea. I later found out that he was the head of the Society of Vedanta, a Hindu organization strongly assertive in matters of spiritual religion. His headquarters in Boston radiated a sort of benign stimulation. Once he took me upstairs and told me that he wanted to share an experience. We stood in front of a wooden cabinet in which he said was a relic of the great Hindu saint Ramakrishna. I felt a strange uplifting stimulation that lasted for several days.

He was held in great respect and esteem by the philosophic and religious elements in the Boston community. Once a year he would stage a banquet attended by several hundred invited guests, held in honor of the birthday of his great teacher. I once remarked to him that all these people had no interest in Ramakrishna, but came out of respect for him. He smiled his acknowledgment. He and I were frequent visitors at the home of Professor Sorokin in Winchester, where we planned the Research Society in Creative Altruism. He would personally serve a tasty preparation of rice that he had prepared pursuant to his early vocation as a cook. At every religious luncheon, he was regularly invited to ask grace, and he always ended his short invocation with the words, "Peace, peace, peace." His smiling demeanor radiated this sentiment. He took an active part in the organization of the Research Society for Creative Altruism, a development of Professor Sorokin's great work in this field when he was retired from Harvard University. This organization was planned to continue the work of Professor Sorokin's Harvard Foundation for the Creation of Creative Altruism. The Swami deeply deplored the failure of this organization to function, and joined with Professor Walter H. Clark in urging me to reorganize and carry on the work.

His spirituality was deep-seated. He never spoke about "believing" this or that. He knew. I once asked him whether he had ever enjoyed the experience of breaking through and contacting Reality known as mysticism. He said that he had. This gave him an assurance that was stimulating to behold.

He held regular sessions with groups of students. The one at the Massachusetts Institute of Technology was representative of his consuming interest in helping persons with spiritual problems. I recall vividly his concern to help me when I was emotionally shaken by Professor Edwin Booth's sermons extolling constructive action at the Star Island conferences—which the Swami regularly attended and participated in. A session in which he presided was crowded.

We can almost say that he radiated the peaceful composure that dominated his life. His demeanor never changed. He was always the same cheerful, peaceful Swami. I told him that his assistant had said that India had three million gods. He sniffed his dissent and said that there was only one God. His certainty about religious matters was a continuing inspiration. He said that his great teacher, Ramakrishna, had broken through into direct contact with Reality by following the practices of three religions, among them Hinduism and Christianity.

His replies to all my questions were always given with assurance and not brooking any doubt. When I asked him if there was any evidence of the authenticity of reincarnation, he replied that there were several well-attested cases, and cited the well-known case of the Hindu girl who remembered her previous life and led investigators to the scene. I later found that her name was Shanti Devi.

I never saw any evidence that the Swami influenced the thinking of American religious leaders. His great influence was his appeal to individuals through his sympathy, his gentle manner, and the inspiration of his religious certainty of the authenticity of the religious fundamentals. The services that he held at his headquarters on Sunday mornings were attended by about 75 persons. His messages were delivered in that mood of peace that characterized him. He had a great influence on me to quiet my restless spirit and stimulate me to press on in my spiritual life. His spiritual certainties transcended my beliefs.

Waterville, Vermont

❦

ROBERT ULICH

Instead of summarizing the content of a book, as sometimes happens in introductory comments, I intend to conjure up before the reader's mind the image of the author as I have preserved it in my memory.

The Swami was a highly gifted man of wide international knowledge, but he was not an "intellectual." Rather, he had achieved that inner depth and unity, or that wisdom, which merges the rational and the trans-rational as well as the single items of knowledge into a coherent whole. Hence he possessed that sense of proportion by which he distinguished the important from the unimportant and the essential from the trivial. The single received its meaning from its place in the whole, and the whole was not merely a mass of occurrences, but an embracing, ultimately mysterious reality.

With a smile he listened to, or read about, the discussions of the academic philosophers at the Harvard Faculty Club. He often visited there, perhaps with the feeling that the fights and animosities, which so unfortunately had divided the Christian tradition, had emigrated into the modern "schools of philosophy," such as relativism, pragmatism, idealism, essentialism, existentialism, and other "isms." (Even some of our modern theological departments resemble more a debating society than a seat of faith).

On the other hand, many things for which some of his

learned colleagues believed to have no time were for him significant: the questions of a student, the sexual problems of young men and women, or the turn in a casual conversation where he intuitively felt the inner insecurity in a seemingly well-settled person. He was a teacher in the truest sense of the term, a guide of youth, and a participant in their troubles and aspirations.

The Swami was well trained in the history of Hinduism and Buddhism, as he was acquainted with the history of Christian thought. Having the perspective of a man of different cultures, he could lead a young seeker more deeply into the essence of Judaism and Christianity than many a minister was able to do. He never was a typical "theologian." Dogmas, wonders, and miracles were for him more a hindrance on the way toward unity with the divine than an enrichment. On the other hand, he knew well that, in some persons more than in others, the religious sentiment needed self-expression in the form of cult and symbols, or an aesthetic element, and especially, *mental preparation*. Although he acknowledged the suddenness of religious revelation in some men such as Paul, Francis of Assisi and Ignatius of Loyola, he nevertheless believed that the "inner light" could not be switched on like an electrical bulb. Hence he wrote *Spiritual Practices*. (See especially the chapters on "Requirements for a Spiritual Student and Teacher," also the chapter on "Spiritual Methods").

I never spoke with the Swami about the ecumenical movement. But I guess that he was sorry that it was necessary at all. Being educated in the tolerance of the great Asiatic religions, he saw the *oikumene*, or "the common housing" of the souls of men, in the mystical unity that makes brethren of all in whom the divine spirit, or the sense of the eternal, is alive.

The Swami was not one of those Indian gurus who pretend to heal our uprooted civilization. To be frank, in some of them I have detected a certain vanity. And though, it seems to me, he was well acquainted with Yoga-practices, they were for him not essential.

Without any pose he moved among us simply, modestly,

and naturally, as is evident also in his style of writing. When I met him for the first time I intuitively felt the presence of an unusual personality. He was a lover of life and men. Yet, he wished the multiplicity of human existences to be united by the common conviction that man is not only the creature of men but also of universal forces that reach beyond our scientific knowledge. He was not a dualist, dividing the world into a lower and higher kind of reality, one separated from the other. Religion was for him the achievement of a sense of universal belonging and at the same time of inner freedom that did not demand the sacrifice of the intellect. His mysticism did not contradict but transcended the empirical urge in man.

Thinking of Swami Akhilananda and his friends, I am reminded of an experience I often had at large conferences. I found there that a certain type of men discover each other in the crowd by an instinctive sensitiveness. At Harvard the Swami's friends became acquainted without formal introductions. Some of them did not fit into the departmental niches of "experts." They were esteemed scholars with a great respect for painstaking research, but they were suspicious of mere erudition and somewhat suspect of the intellectual positivists who are afraid of being blamed as "unscientific" when they venture beyond the limits of so-called "empiricism" (sometimes only a word for spiritual timidity). Though perhaps adding something to the mass of knowledge, men of that caliber nevertheless destroy the deeper sources of inspiration without which a culture is bound to perish.

I do not wish to mention individually the members of the circles among whom Akhilananda used to move. Their names are partly to be found in the author's preface and in the context of the book.

The central scheme of Swami's thought was man's search for unity with the Divine. Different persons may achieve this goal by different ways, but certainly one of them has been shown to us in Swami Akhilananda's *Spiritual Practices*.

Harvard University
Cambridge, Massachusetts

ELIHU S. WING, JR.

"Lord, make me an instrument of Thy peace. Where there is hatred, let me sow love; where there is injury, pardon; where there is doubt, faith; where there is despair, hope; where there is darkness, light; where there is sadness, joy."

This familiar prayer of St. Francis of Assisi is an exemplification of the life of Swami Akhilananda.

Swami Akhilananda came to America from India in 1926. His first contact with our family occurred about four years later when he was seen as a patient by my father, Dr. Elihu S. Wing, Sr., in 1930 at the age of thirty-six. Very shortly he became a very special friend of our family, ultimately involving three generations.

Along with many other physicians, my father maintained a close friendship with the Swami and had the pleasure of guiding his medical care for over thirty years. As their friendship grew, I am sure that my father was very early impressed by the depth of Swami's gentle concern and how tirelessly he worked for the good of others. Indeed, he gave of himself so completely that there were times when my father was seriously concerned for the Swami's own health. In fact, his health was variable throughout his life. On some occasions his illnesses were quite critical, and he experienced considerable discomfort and pain. Nevertheless, the God in him spoke continually. His thoughts were entirely toward others and with concern for the undue work his illness was causing the doctors. His humility, even in the face of adversity, was a model to behold. I am sure that many of his friends were totally unaware of the considerable suffering he endured throughout the last four or five years of his life, but inevitably, he found his comfort through the consolation of others.

I am sure that it would be permissible at this date to reveal excerpts of correspondence that took place over twenty years ago regarding the Swami's health. In the early summer of 1948 my father wrote to the President of the Ramakrishna Mission on behalf of Swami Akhilananda as follows:

> Over the past few years I have been conscious of the fact that Swami Akhilananda has been carrying far too heavy a load. He has long looked over-tired and very seldom takes any vacation. He travels frequently and has been doing a great deal of valuable work in connection with several of the local universities. Even during the summer he carries on extensive work for his friends, not to mention the many conferences, committee meetings, and other responsibilities.
>
> As his medical adviser, I write to you, asking if there isn't some way in which the Swami could be given some assistance in carrying this burden. In making this request, I assure you that it is prompted by my initiative and not the request of Swami himself. I am sure that many of his friends would join me in this request. It is our desire to see the Swami keep his health and extend his good work, which is felt not only here in New England, but in many sections of the United States.

In response to this letter my father received a letter from Swami Virajananda in which he stated:

> I was greatly impressed by your solicitude about Swami Akhilananda and also about the cause he represents. I may assure you that we are no less in earnest about sending an assistant to the Swami, but due to the expanding work and demand, it is necessary that some Centers pass through great stress and strain. Can you not kindly persuade the Swami to curtail his activities a little till we can send him someone.

As a result of this letter my father encouraged the Swami to follow the advice of Swami Virajananda and curtail his activities a little. He was advised to try to arrange for a vacation and to limit his working hours so that he might obtain more rest. It had been the Swami's habit to work almost twenty hours a day. In September of 1948 my father was gratified to receive a letter from Atlantic City in which the Swami wrote:

> I know that you will be glad to see my new address. I came here on Friday, September 10th, after the conference on sci-

ence, philosophy, and religion in New York. I am resting very well and doing nothing. You are right. I needed this change and rest, although I did not like to admit it as so many things had to be done. You know I cannot refuse to do some things when the people have so much suffering. However, I am doing what you and others wanted me to.

I have a very nice room facing the ocean. My room is practically surrounded by the ocean. It seems I am on a boat. By the way, you will be amused to know I meet people even here who really need interviews.

So we see again that the Swami, even when at rest and relaxation, could not help but share his thoughts and concerns for others with whom he was in contact. His letters always carried a personal touch and interest for each and every one in the family.

Swami's thoughtfulness was evidenced in many ways. His love for children and their attraction to him was unique. At first, perhaps it was the box of cookies he brought them, but later it was his warm and gentle manner that drew the young folk to him. He exhibited an insight and depth of personal understanding which was tenderly conveyed so that one could discuss anything with him and realize that his interest was sincere.

I would like to strengthen this aspect of the Swami's life by quoting from another letter, this time that of a very close friend of our family.

Swami Akhilananda was first introduced into my life when I was an average youth, displaying rebellion, waywardness, exhibiting free thinking, non-conventionality, and all the perversities that really say, "Leave me alone and let me be myself." I was in mental pain and turmoil because I could not make rational sense out of life. I had even given up my traditional Christian background as it seemed a mockery as compared to Christ's life. The Swami, smilingly and graciously and with great sensitivity answered many questions that I had on a slip of paper, clutched in my hand. When he gently ushered me out with the positive suggestion, "Come again," I knew my life had changed. A door had opened through which light shone, giving me the needed incentive and motivation to build a meaningful bridge to that resented land of adulthood which I had apparently resisted.

This transition was quite painful, slow, and much like a duel. I was wary of this fisher of men, for I knew we were playing for high stakes—one's very soul, and I was in no mood to be humbled to that extent. Yet, slowly, over a period of years, drawn by his loving patience, his deep insight, and his endless admonition to meditate as a solution to any and all problems, I did realize a certain stability and peace of mind I might otherwise not have known. That is a priceless gift I owe to Swami Akhilananda.

My personal contact with Swami began as a young teenager. The Swami frequently visited in our home, both at Providence and in the country. He always enjoyed the peace and quiet of the countryside and all of nature. Although as a youngster I could not quite convince him to go swimming or fishing with me, I know he shared my enthusiasm and joy for these activities. He always had a keen interest in our lives and frequently would talk with us, relating stories of his own boyhood in India. I vividly recall many long summer evenings spent talking with him before a warm fire on a cool night. He seemed to have an inexhaustible well of knowledge and a most charming and convincing way of presenting it to us. During the winter months I occasionally visited the Swami in his Providence Center, frequently with young friends. He also spoke in our church to the young people. He continually encouraged our church relationships and the deepening of our religious practices. While away in school, college, medical school, and the Navy, I received letters from the Swami, speaking of his interest and concern in my activities.

Upon my return to Providence in 1952 I entered the practice of medicine with my father. Swami Akhilananda was one of the first to welcome me home. At this time I introduced him to my wife. They immediately became fast friends. Thus Swami came to be a frequent visitor in our home. I have a most vivid recollection of him, sitting in our living-room with our first young daughter, just a few weeks old, on his lap. In a gentle way he seemed to thrill in talking and playing with her. And so it was with each of our three children as with considerable interest he watched them grow and mature. On the last occasion he was seen in our medical office, Swami particularly asked that we bring to him our youngest baby, then just a few months old. At this time, in spite of his physical pain, he exuded deep warmth and pleasure in holding the young child.

Swami's kindness to our family was not only in his words, but also in his deeds. I well remember several instances of illness in our family when Swami made special trips from Boston to visit. Upon one or two of these visits he brought considerable relief from severe muscle pain by gentle massage.

I recall after one such visit with us when Swami was returning to Boston on a snowy evening with perhaps a little more haste than the law allowed, he was stopped by a policeman. Upon seeing the Swami's clerical collar, the policeman said in his thick Irish brogue: "Get along with ye, Father. I am sure the good Lord will protect ye." The Swami always enjoyed a joke and found it easy to laugh. His inevitable twinkling eyes and ready smile would frequently break forth as he began: "You will be amused to know . . ." and then he would proceed to tell a story.

How can one think of the Swami without remembering the delightful birthday anniversary dinners of Ramakrishna. How lovingly he prepared the food and served it, personally tending to each one's needs. These dinners were always highlighted by inspiring talks given by brother Swamis and friends from the clergy and universities. Throughout all of these activities he maintained a deep spiritual commitment in a totally God-centered life. On several occasions, we as a family had the distinct privilege of partaking in a most meaningful worship service with the Swami. Swami exemplified a depth of spiritual presence which was truly remarkable. He continually encouraged us in our own spiritual practices and devotions. One could not escape the realization of being in the presence of a man of God. He was radiant in his devotion. His life touched many lives, and we will ever be grateful that it touched ours too.

Swami Akhilananda was an instrument in our lives of peace, love, forgiveness, faith, hope, joy, and, above all else, an instrument of God.

Providence, Rhode Island

REVIEWS

R. ANTOINE, S.J.

(A review of Swami Akhilananda's
Hindu View of Christ)

Although written more than twenty years ago, this book has kept much of its relevance. Its central message will be better understood and better received today than in the past because Christian attitudes have undergone considerable changes during the last twenty-five years.

Swami Akhilananda firmly believes that Christ is a divine incarnation, that is, "a person who is thoroughly established in the All-Loving Being, who has no trace of cosmic ignorance, who is completely illumined (namely, who has direct knowledge of God and consequent understanding of the world process), and who understands the meaning and value of historical events." Being always aware of his divine nature, an *avatāra* is not bound by any limitations whatsoever. He appears in the world of ignorance as a beacon of light dispelling the darkness in which ordinary men are at a loss to find their way. Such was Jesus: a Yogi fully integrated in the perfect realization of the fundamental unity which sustains the whole reality. Thus, as the author states, the Hindu will agree with orthodox Christianity, in regarding "Christ as unique in comparison with ordinary men; yet he will differ in holding that there have been and will be numerous incarnations of God."

Broadening the scope of his investigation, the author undertakes to analyse the nature of the religion preached by Christ. In this analysis he shows a rare spiritual wisdom. The core of religion is a direct experience of God or awareness of the divine Presence. "If Bertrand Russell or Sigmund Freud or John B. Watson claims that there is no God, that you and I are mere external appearances in the blind activities of material forces, we have no basis on which to refute the challenge. How do we know that God exists if we have not experienced Him?" The author quotes the words of Swami Vivekananda: "Religion is realization; not talk, nor doctrine, nor theories, however beautiful they may be. It is being and becoming, not hearing or acknowledging; it is the whole soul becoming changed into what it believes. That is religion." (*The Complete Works of Swami Vivekananda* [Mayavati, 1968], Vol. II, p. 396.)

But realization supposes spiritual effort. That is what Jesus taught his disciples. We must beware of certain so-called "spiritual practices" which falsify the very notion of spirituality. As the author says, "Many a man has fallen into the trap of occult, psychic spiritualism in the name of religion." Genuine religious exercises are those which lead us to God through integration of the emotions, will, and thought. To discover the will of God and to do it is the objective of true religion. When the human will is in harmony with the divine will, man is integrated. In order to reach that state of selfless love, one must "purify the ego and cleanse the whole inner attitude." This implies a whole system of habits, ways, and actions; in other words, spiritual practices for the cultivation of divine love. These practices, the author reminds us, "are not mysterious as some critics seem to think. They are not incantations or processes of propitiation of certain deities. They are not allurement of God so that He will shower us with his blessings. Neither are they processes of self-hypnosis. They are mainly a method of cultivation of the thought of God, a method of manifestation of divine love."

Religion, well understood, is not a matter of a few isolated practices reserved for certain days; religion is a transformation of the whole life. As the author says: "Life cannot be divided into secular and spiritual compartments; it must be one or the other . . . What a man makes of his life entirely depends on his attitude. He becomes religious when his attitude is one of awareness of God; and he becomes secular if he does not cultivate that awareness."

The religion of Christ has no place for temporal power and violence. It advocates the inner transformation of man, the control of all lower greeds and tendencies and the manifestation of man's higher self. Christ's death on the Cross is the supreme testimony of the Spirit against brutal force. Aggression and violent conquest are the very denial of Christ's teaching and example. But the world at large is unable to understand the message of Christ's death and history shows that man is more inclined to follow the instinctive voice of violence than to listen to wisdom which says that they who take the sword shall perish with the sword. The real strength of man is his soul force. The example of Christ shows us, as the author points out, that "we must not take any violent step even under provocation nor hate the evil doers, knowing that evil is being done by them because of their ignorance of the higher values of life and because they cannot control their lower nature and impulses of greed, anger, and love of power."

The death of Christ opens the gate to true life. Man may conquer the whole material universe and still remain a slave to his animal instincts. The true conquest which will transform life is the inner conquest. Speaking of the spirit of Easter, the author says: "Jesus demonstrated on Good Friday that we must allow our empirical selves to be crucified in order to conquer the flesh and its cravings. Then alone is there the possibility of changeless immortal life."

When Jesus sent his disciples to go and preach the gospel to every creature, he certainly wanted them to be the messengers of genuine religion. The first qualification of a spiritual teacher is to be spiritually integrated. According to the spiritual maturity of the preacher, two approaches are possible. The author states: "The saving of souls can be done only by illumined personalities of the highest type. The life of Mary Magdalene is an illustration." But for men who are still on the way to perfect integration, the second approach is indicated, namely, the sharing of religious experiences. On this point, the author has anticipated a significant change of attitude in the Christian missionary mind. A deeper knowledge of the spiritual value of other religions has convinced a good number of Christian missionaries that the preaching of religion could not be a monologue, but had to take the form of a dialogue. Since the Spirit of God is at work everywhere, it is vain for any individual or for any group to claim the monopoly of spiritual experience. All men are pilgrims on the way to realization and the Spirit speaks to them in various ways. When they meet, they should meet as pilgrims engaged in a common quest. Instead of wasting time in arguing and refuting one another, they should share their experience and thus enrich one another in their common desire to answer the call of the Spirit. As the author says: "The real representatives of Hinduism, Christianity, and other religions can exchange ideas and ideals and live a life of personal integration. This very method will act as direct and indirect dissemination of religious living. This friendship of the devotees of God belonging to different religions will have a tremendous influence in society." A little further, in his last conclusion, the author writes: "We feel that for the greater good of the world civilization and consciousness of one world, the mutual exchange of ideas and ideals through integrated spiritual personalities is absolutely necessary. Hence, Hindus should welcome Christian missionaries and Christians should welcome Hindu missionaries as co-workers and co-builders of a harmonious civilization." This conclusion should be gladly accepted by all those who have dedicated their lives to the service of Truth.

—*Bulletin* of the Ramakrishna Mission Institute of Culture
   Volume XXIV, Number 3, March, 1973.

KENDIG BRUBAKER CULLY

(A review of Swami Akhilananda's
Spiritual Practices)

With the nascent interest in Eastern religions throughout the West, there will doubtless be a renewed interest in the teachings of Swami Akhilananda. Possibly the posthumous contribution of this Indian religionist will be greater than his fame during his lifetime when the climate was not yet as ready for the Ramakrishna-Vedanta approach.

For Akhilananda "the goal of religion is the attainment of knowledge of the Ultimate Reality and its relationship with finite beings." The "Ultimate Reality" is synonymous, in his thought, with the Absolute, or God, or Holy One, or Allah, or Brahman, or Truth. He does not deny revelation from the Reality, but thinks of spiritual practices as necessary for the preparation of persons for the reception of the revelation.

This volume is both a statement of the rationale for meditational religious experience and an outline of the range of practices available for spirituality. He stresses the need for subjective experiencing, but nowhere condones selfish subjectivism, stating "we need religion not only to satisfy ourselves but also to serve mankind." The effects of meditation, pragmatically, include the strengthening of the mental and physical constitution, the eliminating of nerve tensions, and the imparting of knowledge of God. He believes, also, that society could be made peaceful and harmonious through a wider use of such practices.

No one will find here a complete manual on how-to-do-it lines. This writer offers no easy ten-lesson course, but he provides the groundwork on which any serious student of meditation can build, drawing from many religious traditions, Western as well as Eastern.

—*The Review of Books and Religion*
    Volume 3, Number 1, Mid-September, 1973.

DONALD L. KARR

(A composite review of five books by Swami Akhilananda)

An important part of our "New Age" are spiritual centers scattered throughout the country made up of largely Western followers of Hindu doctrines, disciplines and teachers. Although this has become widespread in the past decade, it has been present since 1893, when Swami Vivekananda, the chief disciple of Sri Ramakrishna, came to the United States and founded the first spiritual centers in the West called Vedanta Societies.

There are ten of these centers in the country, more than half of them simply called "Vedanta Society," led by resident teachers who are ordained monks from India tracing their initiations back to Ramakrishna. The movement regards Ramakrishna as an avatar and his immediate disciples as important saints. Its main efforts have been in presenting the Vedanta as a universal religion, usually formulating India's basic sacred tradition this way: (1) that man's inner nature is divine (because it is the same, ultimately, as the essence of the Godhead), (2) that the main goal in life is to realize this divine nature (finding the ultimate truth in mystical experience), and (3) that all religions are so many different paths to this goal. The Swamis of the Ramakrishna Order serve as ministers and teachers, sometimes taking disciples. They modestly keep to a minimum any speculation as to whether they may have special spiritual attainments or powers.

Swami Akhilananda lived in this country from 1926 to the time of his death in 1962, and as the head of centers in both Boston and Providence, he was the movement's main representative in New England. He was popular with intellectuals connected with Harvard, Boston University, and Brown, and the Boston and Providence areas in general. Some of these were initiated disciples of his, including even a number of ministers within the Judeo-Christian traditions and others among these intellectuals who were friends. He was a powerful, if quiet, influence on the spiritual life of two urban communities—an influence which is being felt today by people who have never even heard of him.

The Swami's views on various subjects, as found in *Spiritual Practices*, resemble those of his brother monks but are nonetheless in the main his own. He holds that the main answer to individual problems is for people to actively seek God-realization; and that if enough individuals do this, social problems will take care of themselves. The Swami insists that every individual spiritual aspirant must follow a path suited to his own history and needs. He discusses the main types of Yoga—Jnana, Karma, Raja, and Bhakti, and questions the value of obtaining realization quickly. He does grant that an avatar or one of the avatar's close disciples can give realization instantaneously, but this is not the operation of some special technique; even so, continuing spiritual practices are necessary to maintain what has been given.

All five works are collections of sermons released because the Swami's followers wanted them circulated. They are not written with the care with which a book would have been. Of the five, the best edited is probably *Hindu View of Christ*. Had Swami Akhilananda given less of his time to people and more to his writing of books, his genuine intellectual abilities would have been better demonstrated. He deserves better, but we are very fortunate to have the insights of this great teacher available to us.

—*The East West Journal*
Volume III, Number 6, June, 1973.

KENNETH R. WARREN

(A review of Swami Akhilananda's
Spiritual Practices)

This is a modern work on mysticism. Its publication comes at an appropriate time. As so many people, especially of the younger generation, are trying mystical approaches to religion, it behooves us all to try to understand what genuine mysticism is. Swami Akhilananda's thoughts can make a great contribution to such an understanding.

Dean Walter G. Muelder of the Boston University School of Theology in an excellent introduction says, "From all serious and mature religious consciousness [Swami Akhilananda] draws encouragement and offers guidance to those who will experiment in the fruitfulness of meditation . . . He invites minds who are steeped in modern science to begin a spiritual venture which will transform their personalities without betraying their legitimate sophistication." It is not an obscure work coming to us from a remote past. The Swami was active in the Vedanta movement in the United States from 1926 until his death in 1962. He was familiar with many religious traditions and with contemporary scientific knowledge. It is in the language of our time that he reiterates the conviction of the mystics of all ages and places, that religion is the direct and immediate experience of the Ultimate Reality.

"It is our conviction," he says, "that any man or woman—Christian, Hindu, Muslim, Jew, Buddhist, Taoist, agnostic, or atheist—can have spiritual realization, provided he fulfills certain requirements." He lists the requirements. He quotes Swami Vivekananda: real religion is the "manifestation of the divinity that is already in man." One by one he speaks of the steps involved in such manifestation. In simple form and straightforward language he discusses how persons of widely varied points of view may achieve the kind of spiritual growth which he deems essential to an integrated personality and a harmonized society. Reminiscent of *The Practice of the Presence of God* and *The Cloud of Unknowing*, this takes its place as a classic of mysticism; and because it is a modern one, it can help greatly to clarify that much misunderstood word.

One may read it carefully and still not be persuaded that the way of the mystic is the only or even the best avenue to truth, but one cannot read it carefully without gaining a better understanding and a deeper appreciation of mysticism and of a *mahatma*, Swami Akhilananda, a learned yet unassuming, gentle but firm soul, who spoke with simple eloquence of it.

—*Unitarian-Universalist World*
1974.

WRITINGS OF SWAMI AKHILANANDA

"Extra-Sensory and Superconscious Experiences." *The Cultural Heritage of India.* Vol. I: *The Philosophies.* Edited by Haridas Bhattacharyya. 2d ed. Calcutta: The Ramakrishna Mission Institute of Culture, 1953.

Hindu Psychology: Its Meaning for the West. Introduction by Gordon W. Allport and Foreword by Edgar Sheffield Brightman. Boston: Branden Press, 1946.

Hindu View of Christ. Introduction by Walter G. Muelder. Boston: Branden Press, 1949.

Mental Health and Hindu Psychology. Introduction by O. Hobart Mowrer. Boston: Branden Press, 1951.

Modern Problems and Religion. Introduction by Pitirim A. Sorokin. Boston: Branden Press, 1964.

Spiritual Practices. Introduction by Walter G. Muelder. Boston: Branden Press, 1972.

Spiritual Practices. Memorial Edition with Reminiscences. Edited by Alice May Stark and Claude Alan Stark. Cape Cod, Mass.: Claude Stark, Inc., 1974.

Sri Ramakrishna and Modern Psychology. Providence: The Vedanta Society, 1937.

"Values of Life." *Vedanta for Modern Man.* Edited by Christopher Isherwood. New York: Collier Books, 1962.

CONTRIBUTORS

SWAMI ASESHANANDA is spiritual leader of the Vedanta Society of Portland, Oregon, and a senior monastic member of the Ramakrishna Order of India.

PETER A. BERTOCCI is Borden Parker Bowne Professor of Philosophy, Boston University.

BETTY A. BOGERT is a Christian minister and painter, living in Lisbon, New Hampshire.

The late EDWIN P. BOOTH was Professor Emeritus of Historical Theology, Boston University School of Theology.

RALPH WENDELL BURHOE is Editor of *Zygon: Journal of Religion and Science,* Chicago, Illinois, and was formerly Executive Officer of the American Academy of Arts and Sciences.

AMIYA CHAKRAVARTY is Professor of Philosophy at State University College, New Paltz, New York, and Professor Emeritus of Comparative Oriental Religions and Literature, Boston University School of Theology. He was secretary to Rabindranath Tagore.

WALTER HOUSTON CLARK is Professor Emeritus of the Psychology of Religion, Andover Newton Theological School and former Dean of the Hartford School of Religious Education, Hartford Seminary Foundation.

KENDIG BRUBAKER CULLY is Editor of *The Review of Books and Religion* and former Dean and Professor of Religious Education, New York Theological Seminary.

L. HAROLD DeWOLF is former Dean and Professor of Systematic Theology, Wesley Theological Seminary and former Professor of Systematic Theology, Boston University School of Theology.

DANA L. FARNSWORTH is Director of University Health Services, Harvard University, and a consultant on psychiatry.

CLARENCE H. FAUST was Dean of the College, University of Chicago, also its Acting President, and was Vice President of the Ford Foundation. He now resides in Claremont, California.

SRIMATA GAYATRI DEVI is spiritual leader of the Vedanta Centre in Cohasset, Massachusetts and of the Ananda Ashrama, La Crescenta, California, which celebrated its fiftieth anniversary last year.

DANA McLEAN GREELEY is minister of the First Parish Church in Concord, Massachusetts. He was President of the Unitarian-Universalist Association of North America, 1958-1969.

PAUL E. JOHNSON is Professor Emeritus of the Psychology of Religion, Boston University School of Theology.

JOHN H. LAVELY is Professor of Philosophy and Chairman of the Department of Philosophy, Boston University.

RICHARD M. MILLARD is Director of Higher Education Services, Education Commission of the States and former Dean of the College of Liberal Arts, Boston University.

CAROLE MOREAU is a writer residing in Barrington, Rhode Island.

WALTER GEORGE MUELDER is Professor Emeritus of Christian Social Ethics and Dean Emeritus of Boston University School of Theology. He was Dean of the School from 1945 to 1972.

JANNETTE E. NEWHALL is Professor Emeritus of Research Methods and former Librarian, Boston University School of Theology.

F. S. C. NORTHROP is Sterling Professor Emeritus of Philosophy and Law, Yale University.

SWAMI PRABHAVANANDA is spiritual leader of the Vedanta Society of Southern California and a senior monastic member of the Ramakrishna Order of India.

S. PAUL SCHILLING is Professor Emeritus of Systematic Theology, Boston University School of Theology. He was also Professor of Systematic Theology at Wesley Theological Seminary.

JAMES HOUSTON SHRADER is Professor Emeritus of Chemistry, Eastern Nazarene College.

CLAUDE ALAN STARK is a research scholar in world religions and Chairman of a development company in Africa.

ROBERT ULICH is Professor Emeritus of Education, Harvard University, and currently resides in Stuttgart, Germany.

KENNETH R. WARREN is minister of the Unitarian-Universalist Church, Barnstable, Massachusetts.

ELIHU S. WING, JR. is a physician in Providence, Rhode Island. His father was Swami Akhilananda's personal physician.

Editors' Note

The Editors wish to express their profound gratitude to the contributors cited above. It is regretted that other intimate friends of the Swami Akhilananda in America such as Edgar S. Brightman, Pitirim Sorokin, Harlow Shapley, Gordon Allport, Henry Cadbury, and the Swamis Ashokananda and Vishwananda are no longer living to contribute their personal recollections of their friendship with him.

Any friends of Swami Akhilananda who may have been overlooked as contributors to this Memorial Edition are invited to submit their reminiscences to the publisher for inclusion in future editions.